Qi
HEALING

The Way to a New Mind and Body

TOSHIHIKO YAYAMA, M.D.

Translated by Chiho Ono-Krag

KODANSHA INTERNATIONAL
Tokyo • New York • London

NOTES TO THE READER

This book is presented as an aid to understanding the theories and practices associated with the use of *qi* energy healing and is not intended to replace medical consultation and treatment. Please consult a doctor or other appropriate health care professional if you are in need of medical treatment. Neither the author nor the publisher may be found liable for any adverse effects or consequences resulting from following any of the advice or instructions in this book.

Please direct any inquiries about tools for *qi* control to: The Cosmic Energy Research Institute, 6-8-3 Nabeshima, Saga, Kyushu, Japan 849-0937.

TRANSLATOR'S ACKNOWLEDGMENT

The translator wishes to thank Carmen Agredo, who read the first draft and made many excellent suggestions, and Dr. Werner Krag, whose explanation and clarification of numerous medical and physiological concepts and expressions were invaluable.

Originally published as *Ki no ningen-gaku*. Tokyo: Bijinesu-sha, 1993.

Distributed in the United States by Kodansha America, Inc., 575 Lexington Avenue, New York, New York 10022, and in the United Kingdom and continental Europe by Kodansha Europe Ltd., 95 Aldwych, London WC2B 4JF.

Published by Kodansha International Ltd., 17-14 Otowa 1-chome, Bunkyo-ku, Tokyo 112-8652, and Kodansha America, Inc.

Copyright © 1999 by Toshihiko Yayama. English translation copyright © 1999 by Kodansha International. All rights reserved. Printed in Japan.

ISBN 4-7700-2382-0

First edition, 1999
99 00 01 02 03 10 9 8 7 6 5 4 3 2 1

Library of Congress Cataloging-in-Publication Data
Yayama, Toshihiko, 1952–
  [Ki no ningen-gaku. English]
  Qi healing: the way to a new mind and body / Toshihiko Yayama; translated by Chiho Ono-Krag.
  p.   cm.
  ISBN 4-7700-2382-0 (paperback)
  1. Ch' i kung. 2. Exercise therapy. I. Title.
  RA781.8.Y3913 1999
  613.7'1—dc21   98-52760

C O N T E N T S

Preface

I studied modern Western medicine at Kyushu University and, during the course of my graduate study, taught myself to think in a scientific way. I now practice medicine at the prefectural hospital in Saga, Japan, where I am in charge of the departments of Surgery and Oriental Medicine.

You might wonder how someone with a background in "scientific thought" could have happened into the world of *qi*—which is likely at first glance to give a rather heretical and unscientific impression. I hope that my story will convince you of the tremendous power of *qi* energy.

I was interested in psychosomatics—or the branch of medical science that attempts to view body and mind as a network of linked processes—while I was a medical student, but my aim was to become a surgeon. I decided to work in an emergency ward, since emergency surgery is widely known as a specialization that involves considerable use of—experimentation with, if you will—ultramodern medical technology. I underwent a tough period of training there, under the head of the emergency surgery department, who had studied in the United States.

I faced greater difficulties when I entered the internal medicine department, where I saw patients with ailments of all kinds. Many complained of multiple health problems—none of which, however, could be pinpointed even after a lengthy series of examinations. I often found myself unable to offer any practical help. For people who suffered from general health problems, I often could find nothing wrong with them, and so simply prescribed a combination of tranquilizers and vitamins. I gave steroids to those with incurable illnesses like collagen disease. I advised these patients to resign themselves to their condition, and to learn to live with it as well as they could. I felt helpless and wondered if I was actually helping people.

Because of my doubts and concerns about the help I was giving, I began to study Chinese medicine. This brought one revelation after another. For instance, this field taught that there was no such thing as a "general malaise"; any disorder was in fact particular and specific.

The language of Western and Chinese medicine is completely different. The entire concept of *qi*, or "vitality," lies beyond the realm of what is acceptable to Western medical practitioners, since it cannot be checked scientifically; and in the Western tradition, patients are generally diagnosed in keeping with such objective information as numbers shown on machines or the results of X-ray photos. The language of Chinese medicine, on the other hand, allows a caregiver to "read" a patient's *qi*, blood, and water—none of which is possible with Western medicine. Practitioners in this tradition consider serious diseases to be caused by severe blockages of *qi* flow.

Chinese herbs can be helpful after operations, in shortening the time needed for recovery. My interest in Chinese medicine soon led me to learn acupuncture as well. The more familiar I became with various forms of traditional Eastern medicine, the more patients who felt that modern Western medicine had failed them came to see me.

Another problem occurred. I found that I tired very easily whenever I worked in the department of Chinese medicine. This was unusual for me. I had been training in the martial arts day in and day out since I was a teenager and I had every confidence in my health. I kept asking myself what it was that was making me so tired.

It didn't take long to find the cause. I started thinking that as a *qi* practitioner I was actually absorbing negative *qi* energy from my patients. Practice of martial arts increases our *qi* power, but at the same time also increases our sensitivity to *qi*. It is known that the better cancer specialists are at particularly high risk for contracting cancer themselves, and that many psychiatrists suffer from burnout syndrome or depression. These symptoms seem to be caused by an exchange of *qi* between patients and doctors.

Meanwhile I went to a conference on Chinese medicine, where I happened to see a poster about the benefits of *qigong*. Next I had opportunity to meet a *qigong* master—the brain surgeon Yang Zi-Zheng, who became interested in *qigong* as a result of his martial arts training. He encouraged me, as soon as we met. He told me that I would be able to treat patients with "external *qi*" and he actually demonstrated to me the presence and power of external *qi*. He said that the *qigong* method was capable of ridding the world of all disease. That was the day when I began my journey to the *qi* world. I looked for all sorts of documents on *qi* in libraries and at bookstores that handled antique books. I brought my years of training in the martial arts to bear as I tried all the *qi* exercises myself.

Finally I organized my own system of *qigong* exercise sessions. These were for patients who were dissatisfied with the results of their treatment with Western medicine. Looking back on it now, those early *qigong* exercises that I did were quite "primitive." Some patients were too weak to perform the movements. Some were completely unused to exercise. It was obvious that I needed to continue my studies, so that I could develop an approach that would be better suited to the needs of a wider range of patients. For this reason, I think of those early patients as having been my teachers. They taught me what it was I needed to do next.

My academic teachers used to say, "Keep an eye on the past. Stand where you are now. Move into the future." This attitude was what led me to study classical documents while also always experimenting, in an effort to find new approaches. Through perseverance I was able to develop what I call the "Microcosmic Orbit method"—a powerful combination of healing *qigong* exercises. But I still wanted to do more. As a *qi* practitioner involved in treating patients, I needed to go beyond *qigong* exercises altogether. Finally I went on to develop a system that is powerful enough to provide patients with the relief they seek. This book will tell you, step by step, how you too can enter the world of *qi*—how you can be healed, and how you can heal others.

PART ONE
Healing Yourself

I — Our Bodies Are Made of Energy

Learn Qigong

To begin at the very beginning, then, what is *qigong* (pronounced "cheegong")?

I always say to my patients, "*Qigong* is like cooking. Just try following the recipe, and you'll find that you can cook." You can't measure taste with a machine or express it in numbers, but you can experience it for yourself and know, without any doubt, what it is. Likewise, you develop your *qi* ability through the "*qi* feeling" that is as sharp and real as any of your other senses. When your ability is sufficiently developed, you will be able to evaluate your own level, as well as other people's levels.

When you have trained for a long time in the martial arts, you become accustomed to sizing up an opponent before a match, using all your powers of observation and intuition to try to appraise his actual condition and power. Although animals are equipped with this basic survival instinct, humans don't have much of an opportunity to use it anymore, in the modern world. However, when you want to learn something quickly, experimenting is often very useful, and can sometimes lead you to a shortcut. The best way to familiarize yourself with the *qi* world is to experience and release *qi* yourself. I think of myself not as a teacher, but as something like a chef with a fair amount of experience in "cooking with *qi*." My role, as I see it, in this book is simply to guide you and show you how to handle *qi* with confidence.

Qigong arose from the martial arts, the field of medicine, esoteric Buddhism, Taoism, and Yoga. To establish my own *qigong* method, I discarded all the more doctrinaire parts of these traditions and retained only the practical techniques for development of mind and body.

The *qigong* contained in this book is based on the martial arts, which I have practiced for a long time; Chinese medicine, which I have spent many years studying in my work as a physician; Xian-Dao, one of the original sources of Chinese medicine; psychosomatics, which I have studied with great interest since I was in medical school; the ascetic exercises of esoteric Buddhism; and the theories of transpersonal psychology and parapsychology. I borrowed elements from all these traditions, and used all that I have learned in my studies and practice with patients and friends, in creating my system of *qi* healing.

A Living Energy Field

Electric eels have electromagnetic fields around their bodies that they use to catch their prey. In 1958 Dr. Lissman of Cambridge University surprised people when he was able to catch a fish using a magnet.

While studying freshwater fish in Africa, he came upon a specimen of knife fish that measured 1.6 meters in length. The doctor placed a powerful horseshoe-shaped magnet on the surface of the water and the fish swam toward it. When the doctor moved the magnet the fish followed after (Figure 1–1).

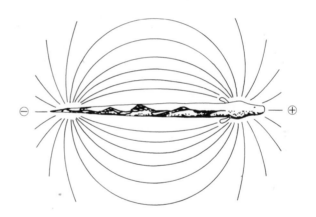

Figure 1–1
Knife fish are known to produce an electromagnetic field around their bodies.

Lissman investigated further, and found that this kind of fish produces an electromagnetic field around its body. The fish was intermittently releasing three to five volts, at frequencies of up to 300 times per second. The fish also showed a great sensitivity to electrical charge, and reacted to even minuscule changes in electric potential. Many electric fish are now known to be surrounded by an electromagnetic field that they use to catch prey, communicate with one another, or protect themselves from predators.

Animals including pigeons, bees, sharks, and dolphins seem to have biological magnets in their bodies, which they use to receive magnetic information from the environment.

What about human beings? In 1961, Robert O. Becker, M.D., a

pioneer in the study of electrical currents in living things, discovered that the magnetic storms of the sun cause disorders in the earth's magnetic field. This in turn was found to worsen the symptoms of schizophrenia in people who suffer from the disease.

Today, magnetic disorder is known to be closely correlated with poor functioning of the autonomic nervous system and aggravation of diseases of the heart and circulatory system, stomach ulcers, and rheumatism. Experiments with mice show that when these animals are completely isolated from the magnetic field, they die within six months. It has also been reported that the brain waves of monkeys adjust quickly to any change in the rhythms of the environmental electromagnetic field, and that these brain wave changes are accompanied by behavioral changes as well.

It is possible to determine whether electromagnetic energy is being released from the body at any given time, by means of a superconducting quantum interference device. This device, which provides magnetic diagrams of the brain and heart, on the basis of electric phenomena, is sometimes used in the study of brain diseases or psychic functioning. All living creatures seem to sense and also to form electromagnetic fields around them, although they are likely not to be aware of these processes.

Harold Saxton Burr, professor of anatomy at Yale University, has conducted brilliant studies on the electromagnetic fields of living creatures. In his experiments, using a simple instrument consisting of vacuum tubes, he discovered that the skin of various animals—including the helminth, the hydra, and the giant salamander—produces a slight electric potential. In addition, he hung a voltameter from a tree which registered changes in the energy field occurring in response to conditions of light, humidity, storms, sunspots, and the waxing and waning of the moon.

Burr notes, "Animals and plants are essentially electric. They show different voltage when they engage in different forms of ordinary biological behavior." He studied the energy in various life forms and reported on the bioelectric character of such basic processes as menstruation, ovulation, sleep, growth, illness, and healing. He emphasized that an energy field surrounds—like a larger and intangible skin—every living creature, helping to maintain its biological structure.

Isn't it time that we began to research and expand on his studies, using today's more refined measuring instruments? We human beings have never been surrounded by so much electromagnetic energy as we are at this point in history. Today we also face unprecedented electromagnetic pollution. Pregnant women working with video or computer monitors run an increased risk of miscarriage or of having a stillborn baby or one suffering from birth defects.

The practice of *qigong* increases our sensitivity to the electromagnetic field. When you have been practicing for some time, you may find, for instance, that if you sit in front of a large television screen or transformer for many hours, you can feel the negative effect it is having on your *qi* flow. Master Morihei Ueshiba, founder of Aikido, is said to have disliked taking trains. His sensitivity and susceptibility must have been so great that he could feel electromagnetic disturbances that are imperceptible to ordinary people.

The Pineal Gland as a Sensor of Qi

How, and with which parts of their bodies, do living creatures sense changes in the electromagnetic field? Here I would like to introduce an interesting experiment: A tiny electrode was inserted into the pineal gland of the exposed brain of a guinea pig, and a helmholtz coil was set around the animal's head. We then created an artificial magnetic field, and checked the reaction of the nerve cells in the pineal gland. The amount of electric discharge was seen to change with changes to the magnetic field (Figure 1–2). This reaction was visible only in the pineal gland, leading us to deduce that the pineal gland reacts to the magnetic field.

Figure 1–2

Magnetic stimulation causes a change in the electric discharge from the pineal gland.

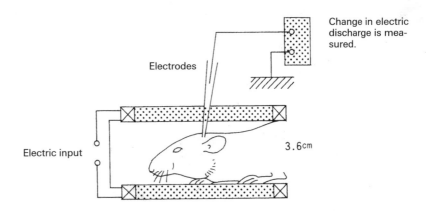

The pineal gland is a small structure projecting from the midbrain (diencephalon) to the back in vertebrates (Figure 1–3). In fish, amphibians, and reptiles, it is thought to play a role in response to light. It secretes a hormone called melatonin and controls the function of reproduction. In birds, the pineal gland controls circadian rhythms and is probably involved in their flight navigation by providing information on the direction of the sunlight and the magnetism of the earth.

In the case of human beings, the Yin-Tang (an acupuncture point

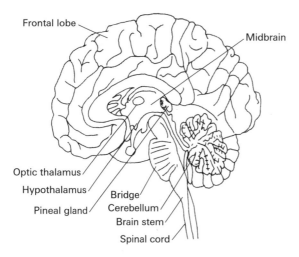

Figure 1–3
Brain anatomy.

Labels: Frontal lobe, Midbrain, Optic thalamus, Hypothalamus, Bridge, Pineal gland, Cerebellum, Brain stem, Spinal cord

on the forehead) is thought to interact with the pineal gland. This acupuncture point is known as Ajina-Chakra in Yoga, and Hui-Yan, meaning "discerning eyes," in the philosophy known as Xian Dao (a form of Taoism). This so-called "third eye" is a very important element in *qigong* training. Practicing these *qigong* exercises will make it possible to let *qi* in or out with a *qi* ball through the Ajina-Chakra by stimulating this point.

Discover the small universe within you. All living creatures have their own energy fields, and not only receive electromagnetic energy from various sources but are also unconsciously influenced by this kind of energy. There is in fact a way to prove the existence of this energy, which should easily convince even people who are not familiar with *qigong*.

Sudden changes in muscle strength occur can be caused not only by physical or chemical stimuli applied to the body but also by more subtle stimuli or information that is not normally perceived by the ordinary senses. The test that I call the "Reflection of *Qi* Muscle Power" is based on this phenomenon (for a more detailed discussion of this test, see Chapter VII, "Kinesiology"). In Western countries, it is known that an immediate decrease in muscle strength follows the application of light pressure to an unwell part of the body, and kinesology is adapted as supplemental diagnosis.

What exactly is meant by the phrase "reflection of *qi* muscle power"? When the subtle energy of the body, or *qi* energy, is activated and promoted, an accompanying increase in muscle power is also seen. By contrast, when *qi* energy declines or stagnates, muscle power decreases. Anything can serve as a stimulus and influence *qi*. The mechanism of "muscle reflection" is not yet totally understood, but it is a recurring phenomenon, and we can vividly sense the existence of *qi* and can also do research to facilitate our further understanding.

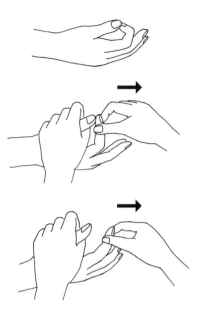

Figure 1–4

Figure 1–4 shows the steps involved in the test.

1. The patient forms a circle with the thumb and index finger of one hand.

2. The tester grips the patient's hand firmly.

3. The tester then grips the patient's index finger. At that point the patient must increase his or her finger power to maintain the circle; the tester pulls on the circle in an effort to gauge the amount of force required to pull the circle apart.

Try performing the test under each of the following conditions:

1. With the patient's other hand held close to a computer screen that has been switched on;

2. With a magnet attached to the patient's hand or body;

3. With some medicine placed on the patient's body. For example, try the test first with one aspirin tablet placed on the pit of the patient's stomach, and then try it again with two or three tablets; and

4. With a cellular phone that has been switched on held in the patient's other hand. The test should be done first with the patient's arm stretched straight out, and then several more times, each time with the arm pulled in about ten centimeters closer to the ear.

Most patients show a reduction in finger strength after performing this test.

If you are a practitioner of *qigong* or the martial arts, try the Reflection of *Qi* Muscle Power test again immediately after practice. Most people find that training does not significantly reduce finger power. In fact I believe that training in *qigong* or the martial arts actually stimulates the circulation of *qi* and of the blood, helping to prevent the *qi* stagnation that can result from exposure to negative or unhealthy stimuli.

The results of the Reflection of *Qi* Muscle Power test differ from one individual to another. Results are also clearer for some people than for others. The tests that I have conducted on many people suggest that people who lead a healthy life and have a positive attitude toward the future seem to show more obvious reactions. Some people tend not to show any clear results from this testing; this group often includes people suffering from stress or exhaustion, as well as those who insist on following only the old and established scientific models.

The results of the Reflection of *Qi* Muscle Power test are reproducible as an input system of *qi* information, and this test is also very effective as a way of achieving greater *qi* power. This test is crucial for those who want to increase their powers of perception through *qigong*.

Even among physicians practicing Western medicine, there is increasing recognition of the effectiveness of stimulating the acupuncture points with a needle, particularly since a method for administering anesthesia by acupuncture was devised. Medical science is gradually coming to accept the idea that the human body has functional points, or acupuncture points. A meridian is a functional line that connects these acupuncture points. The easiest way to feel these meridians for yourself would be to visit an experienced acupuncturist for a session. When the needles penetrate any of the acupuncture points, you will feel a tingling sensation along the meridian. In Chinese, this sense is called "De-Qi," or "obtaining *qi*." This sensation is a sign that the flow of *qi* is being promoted by the needle stimulus. When you practice *qigong*, you will notice this same feeling of De-Qi, but this time throughout a much larger area of your body.

First of all, let's experience *qi* flow with the Reflection of *Qi* Muscle Power test instead of with acupuncture.

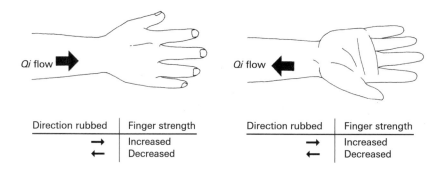

Figure 1–5

Promoting or obstructing the flow of *qi*.

Rub your hand gently about ten times from the elbow to the wrist, on the outer side of the forearm, with your palm facing down, and then try the *Qi* Muscle Power test. Next, rub in the opposite direction (from the wrist to the elbow) and try the test again. Do the same on the other, inner side of the forearm, with your palm facing up. If this is done correctly, you should get the results seen in Figure 1–5.

This reaction is probably caused by the directional quality of the flow of *qi* in the arm. Stimuli that follow the direction of *qi* flow facilitate the flow of *qi*. This in turn strengthens the *qi* muscle power. Stimuli that oppose the flow of *qi* block it. As a result, the ring formed by the thumb and forefinger becomes weaker and opens more easily. You can try this test with your legs, too. Your fingers will open easily or not, depending on the direction in which you rub. Likewise, rubbing your legs in the proper direction can help you recover more quickly when your muscles are sore. If you should get sore leg muscles from, for instance, Standing Zen (see Chapter XIV), try this exercise.

It is important to bear in mind that the flow of *qi* energy is directional.

Invitation to an Unknown World

The "Microcosmic Orbit" is translated from the Chinese "Xiao Zhou Tian," a phrase that points at deep, essential truths. This phrase combines views of the universe and of human beings from Eastern philosophy. It suggests that you yourself are the universe. Like the macrocosmos orbited by *qi* energy, the "inner universe" of the mind and body evolve from the energy orbit. The *qi* around the central meridian has special significance. When you practice the Microcosmic Orbit method, you will come to understand the origin of its name. Once you do, you will

Figure 1–6
LEFT: Du Channel (back channel)
RIGHT: Ren Channel (front channel)

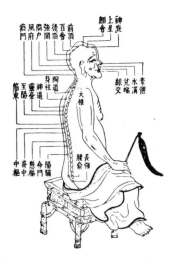
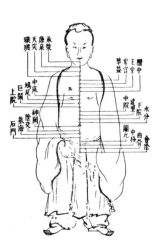

also recognize that you are part of a holonic structure (to borrow a term that was coined in 1970 by Arthur Koestler) that extends from the level of cells to the level of the spirit. It is also clear that you will attain constant, continuing power and ability simply from the awareness that you are the universe.

Before getting into the practical details of "*qigong* cooking" in the style that I have developed, I do want to explain a bit more about the body's main meridians, since this knowledge is basic to further understanding.

There are twelve meridians circling through the human body. These are divided into six Yang (Chinese; "positive") meridians that circle through the back of the body, and six Yin (Chinese; "negative") meridians on the front. *Qi* circulates around the Du (Chinese; "governor") and Ren (Chinese; "conception") channels. The Du Channel controls the six Yang meridians, while the Ren Channel controls the six Yin meridians (Figure 1–6).

II — Welcome To The World of Qi

The Microcosmic Orbit Method

The human body begins to form at the moment that an ovum is fertilized. First to develop is the spinal cord, including that portion at the top that will become the brain. This means that the central nervous system—which will function as a kind of control center in the human body—develops first: peripheral parts then follow symmetrically (Figure 2–1). There are vital points running from the top of the head to the groin along a line at the center of the body in not only newborn babies but also in developing fetuses. In martial arts, this center line is supposed to contain various vital points that are especially important in attacking or protecting. In Eastern medicine, too, this center line on the back and the front of the human body is considered important for many reasons in diagnosis and treatment. People seem to have known intuitively for some time that the center line of the human body is the site of important energy routes.

Figure 2–1
Various stages in the development of an embryo.

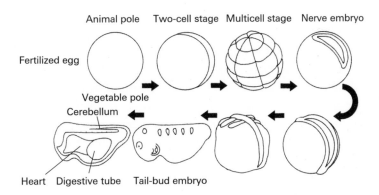

21

As I explained in the previous chapter, these energy routes are the Du Channel for the center line of the back of the human body, and the Ren Channel for the front. In the Microcosmic Orbit method, you will circulate *qi* through the Du and Ren channels. If the route is described anatomically, the Du Channel includes the spinal cord, the adrenal glands, the hypothalamus, and the pituitary gland, all of which are the main centers controlling the functions of the intestines and the hormones. Along the Ren Channel lie the thyroid, thymus, pancreas, celiac plexus, and the gonads, or the main organs of the autonomic nervous system (Figure 2–2).

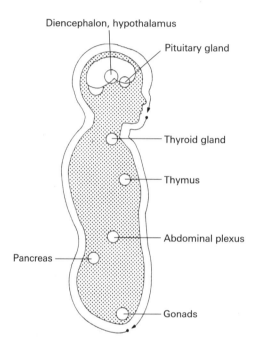

Figure 2–2
Anatomical structure of the Microcosmic Orbit.

Modern biological research has shown that these autonomic functions can be controlled by the power of the mind using biofeedback. It is also known that some Yoga masters are able to easily control their autonomic functions. In Yoga this is done by developing Chakras. In *qigong*, one can use *qi* instead, and reach that same level by practicing the Microcosmic Orbit method. When the autonomic nervous system is developed by means of the Microcosmic Orbit, it becomes possible for all kinds of illnesses to be healed—a result which is not remarkable or strange from the Western medical point of view, but which to the best of my knowledge is never mentioned in classical Chinese medical texts.

When *qi* is able to circulate well through the Ren and Du channels that control the twelve meridians, problems of *qi* blockage are solved. But how does this work? As I said, the method does not seem to be explained in classical Chinese medical texts. However, the Du and the Ren channels cross right on the acupuncture points on the center line of the twelve meridians. These junctures include the Da-Zhui, Bai-Hui, Chong-Wan, and Guan-Yuan. Compare the diagrams of the twelve meridians, and then add the Du and Ren channels. According to my experience, if you allow *qi* to flow freely through the acupuncture points of the Du and Ren channels, *qi* blockages in any of the twelve meridians will disappear. In fact, people whose circulation through the Du and Ren channels is good—in other words, those who master the Microcosmic Orbit method—will no longer experience any blockage of *qi* (see Figure 2–3).

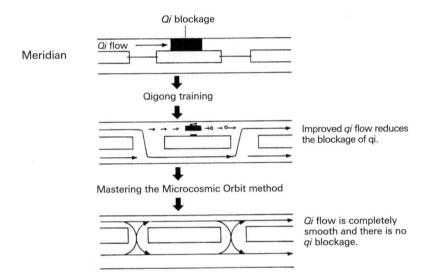

Figure 2–3
Qigong training opens blocked meridians.

How to master the Microcosmic Orbit method

1. Make your backbone straight, flexible, and strong.
2. Comprehend the reality of *qi* and of the "*qi* ball."
3. Learn techniques for strengthening and moving the *qi* ball.
4. Activate first the downward meridian, and then the upward.
5. In men, *qi* usually circles upward through the Du Channel and downward through the Ren Channel. For women, the flow of *qi* is usually opposite: downward through the Du, and upward through the Ren, channels.
6. The "Cosmic Headband" (see Chapter IV), which I invented, can be used if you should want to master the Microcosmic Orbit method quickly.
7. Ask for help from people who have already mastered the Microcosmic Orbit method, so that you can master it quickly.

Making a Qi Ball

Perhaps the most important and basic element in the practice of *qigong* is your own experience of sensing *qi*. Even if you are able to impress others with the most spectacular movements when you perform *qigong* exercises, if you were unable to comprehend *qi* yourself, this would not actually qualify as *qigong*. This is probably the single biggest difference between *qigong* and the martial arts or other exercises such as gymnastics.

The quickest way to learn how to sense *qi* involves learning to make a *qi* ball between your palms with *qi* energy. If you are full of *qi* energy, you will sense warmth, a feeling like the repulsion produced by two magnets, or minute, tingling vibrations in your palms. If you lack *qi* energy, it will be difficult to feel anything right away.

Imagine that your Lao-Gong points and your fingertips are all connected with *qi*.

Figure 2–4
Making a *qi* ball.

Release your consciousness of the *qi* connecting your fingertips, and make a *qi* ball.

How to make a *qi* ball

1. First, form the shape of a ball with the fingertips of both your hands touching (thumb to thumb, forefinger to forefinger, etc.), as if you were holding a baseball.

2. Now, pull your hands apart slowly. Maintain a slight distance (about 5 millimeters) between your fingertips. Imagine that you have only thumbs. Concentrating your mind at the tips of your thumbs, move your thumbs gently. Repeat this movement with the rest of your fingers one by one, then with two fingers together, and then with three and four, and finally all the fingers.

   You may feel a tingling sensation in your fingertips, or

you may feel as if your fingertips were connected with invisible india rubber. This means that you are nearly aware of *qi*.

3. When your thumbs and fingers are all connected with *qi*, keep moving them slowly. This will increase the *qi* sensation between your palms. When you move your thumb and the little finger of one hand, so that they form a circle without touching, you may feel a tingling or some tension in the center of your palm. This is the acupuncture point known as Lao-Gong. You might have more difficulty connecting these points than in connecting your thumbs and fingers. But these are very important points, through which you can absorb or release *qi*. Be perseverant. When your thumbs, all your fingers, and the Lao-Gong points are connected with *qi*, you can increase your *qi* sensation by moving your hands, thumbs, and fingers slowly.

4. Next, release the consciousness of *qi* that was connecting your thumbs, fingertips, and the Lao-Gong points. You should be able to sense an invisible *qi* ball between your palms (Figure 2–4). When this *qi* ball is strengthened with the exercises of the Micro/Macrocosmic Orbit methods, you will see a hazy ball of light between your fingers or palms. This is most likely caused by photons, which relate to biotic phenomena and functions.

    Don't worry, though, if you don't see anything. You've just started, and many people cannot see anything at the beginning. The important thing here is to take it easy and enjoy your experiences.

If your training in *qigong* exercises is effective, you may begin to see things that were invisible before. You may begin to feel things you have never felt before. What's more, when you start using external *qi*, you may discover that you have various paranormal abilities. All these things are quite natural in the world of *qigong*. But I must warn you that these developments can become obstacles to further development, if you take too much pride in your new, unusual abilities. Stay modest!

Straightening Your Spine

We human beings usually suffer from the gradual curving of our backbones, from the time we first begin walking upright, partly because our heads are so heavy relative to the rest of our bodies. The curvature of our backbones tends to damage the autonomic nerve system that branches out from the spine, and to cause various diseases. For example, patients with whiplash injury are likely to suffer for a long time from cervical pain, eye strain, buzzing in the ears, sensations of a stuffed nose or of an obstructed pharynx, palpitations, and other symptoms.

When I examine patients, using my fingers as a *qi* sensor, I can sense when their cervical vertebrae are abnormally curved. But curvature of this sort can be treated with the *qigong* method, by releasing external *qi*. With this treatment, these various complaints begin to disappear. From a *qigong* point of view, it means that the blockage of *qi* at the Du Channel has been removed. In the language of Western medicine, the sympathetic trunk (stellate ganglion), which works as a relay station for the autonomic nerves of the cervix, has been normalized.

The body is like a vessel through which *qi* flows. If the backbone is not straight, *qi* energy cannot flow. Practice of the Microcosmic Orbit method which I systematized allows your *qi* energy to flow smoothly. The exercises in this method include rhythmical swinging and twisting movements. In developing this method of *qigong*, I was most heavily influenced by the Chinese *qigong* called "Wu Qing Xi" (Chinese; "five animals movements") and "Gui She" (Chinese; "turtle and snake"), both of which were systematized by Master Zhou Nian-Feng and are *qigong* methods that imitate the movements of animals.

III — The New Qigong

The Abdominal Breathing Method

If you are like most people, you are probably unaware of the extent to which the way you inhale and exhale affects your energy level. But breathing has long been considered essential to the exercises of the East. For instance, Yoga teachings include many different ways of breathing. One is "Bhastrika," known in English as "breathing of fire," whose aim is to stimulate the fundamental "Kundalini" energy. Likewise, Zen has its technique of "Su Soku Kan" (Japanese; "meditating while counting the number of breaths taken").

Several different breathing methods are used in *qigong*. The ancients seem to have known intuitively that breathing conditions were related to autonomic functioning.

Our breathing changes in keeping with our emotions such as joy, anger, or sorrow. You breathe differently when you are laughing or crying. It's not possible to breathe the same way while crying, as while laughing. If you become too nervous before an exam, say, or a game, and your breathing is influenced, you are not likely to get a good result. Breathing can affect the emotional and the mental state. Many breathing methods are now promoted that seek to control feelings, mind activities, and even vital energy.

In the human body, only breathing is controlled, under normal conditions, by both voluntary and involuntary nerves. This is one of the reasons why the involuntary nerves can be consciously controlled by controlling breathing. After all, breathing can become a bridge between consciousness and unconsciousness.

Improved breathing methods are effective in improving blood circulation. Proper breathing promotes the flow back through your veins and the circulation of blood through the whole body, by changing abdominal pressure. Practicing breathing is an important element of *qigong* training, but it is also important not to try too hard and not to try to do too much too soon.

The following is the breathing method that I recommend as most effective, because I still find it as useful as I did when I first tried it many years ago.

The Raku-raku method of deep breathing

1. Exhale slowly with your mouth open, as if you were yawning.
2. Pause.
3. Exhale slowly through rounded lips, as if you were blowing out a candle.
4. Pause.
5. Exhale the remaining air from your lungs with three short, quick breaths, through rounded lips.
6. Inhale naturally. I call this the "Raku-raku" deep breathing method (Raku-raku means "easily" in Japanese).

This breathing exercise can be repeated very easily, as many times as you wish. When you exhale with rounded lips, positive pressure occurs just inside the airways. The lungs lie deep inside the body and are not easily cleansed by ordinary breathing. The amount of air which is always left inside the lungs is known, in respiratory physiology, as "residual volume." By exhaling three times, as mentioned above, you can clear away this residual volume.

When you master this breathing method, you will be able to breathe abdominally without effort. Give this method a try sometime, particularly when you are feeling particularly stressed. It will make you feel calm and refreshed.

Making a Qi Ball Through Your Arms

Make a *qi* ball that produces a tingling, or electric, sensation between your palms. Breathe in the *qi* from the *qi* ball from your left arm at the same time as you inhale. Visualize the *qi* ball moving through your left arm and into your right arm as you inhale, and you will experience *qi* sensations moving from your forearm to your elbow, and on to your shoulder (Figure 3–1).

When your ability becomes more advanced, you will only need to inhale once to bring the *qi* ball through your left arm up to the inside of your chest, and to exhale once to bring it down to your right arm. You will need to be able to complete this same movement in the opposite direction as well. When you are able to let the *qi* ball circle through your arms, this means that you have reached the first step.

Hold and strengthen the *qi* ball inside your chest. The Anahata Chakra (from Yoga) can be strengthed this way. These exercises will eventually lead to mastery of the Macrocosmic Orbit method, which will be explained in Part Two.

Figure 3–1

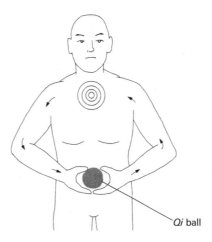

Qi ball

Opening the Microcosmic Orbit

When you have learned to circulate a *qi* ball from your hands through your entire body, you are ready to try the Microcosmic Orbit method. Classical *qi* books ask you to gather *qi* in the lower Dan-Tian and let it flow around your body (Figures 3–2 and 3–3). But it takes too much time to gather *qi* there, and this fact discourages most people from learning the Microcosmic Orbit method. The method I have developed is actually a lot easier than the classic method.

Make a *qi* ball between your palms. Now try to use this *qi* ball to open the meridians of the Microcosmic Orbit in your body.

How to open the Microcosmic Orbit (for men)

1. Strengthen the *qi* ball until you can feel "magnetic pressure," or tingling sensations.

2. Bring the *qi* ball to the crown of your head (Bai-Hui).

3. With your palms turned toward your head, stimulate Bai-Hui with the *qi* ball, as if you were massaging your head, but without touching it. You will feel a light pressure on or tingling sensations in the head.

4. When you feel the *qi* sensations strongly enough, bring the *qi* ball slowly to the acupuncture point between your eyes (Yin-Tang). Stimulate the Yin-Tang with the *qi* ball.

5. Repeat this, bringing the *qi* ball down to the following acupuncture points: Tian-Tu, Tang-Zhong, Zhong-Wang, and Qi-Hai. You will probably feel a coolness or tingling in the Bai-Hui and Yin-Tang, and warm sensations from Tian-Tu through the Qi-Hai.

6. Lead the *qi* ball from Qi-Hai to Xian-Gu through Hui-Yin.

7. Bring the *qi* ball to Ming-Men. Lay your hands on this point until it gets warm.

8. Stimulate from Ling-Tai, Da-Chui, Nao-Fu and back to Bai-Hui.

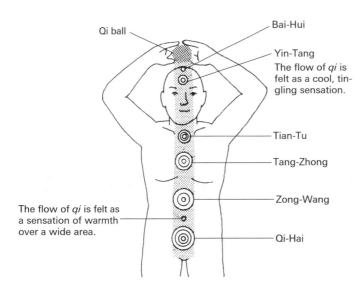

Qi ball

Bai-Hui

Yin-Tang
The flow of *qi* is felt as a cool, tingling sensation.

Tian-Tu

Tang-Zhong

Zong-Wang

The flow of *qi* is felt as a sensation of warmth over a wide area.

Qi-Hai

Figure 3–2
The Ren (front) Channel of the Microcosmic Orbit method.

How to open the Microcosmic Orbit (for women)

1. Strengthen the *qi* ball until you can feel magnetic pressure or tingling sensations.

2. Bring the *qi* ball to the crown of your head.

3. With your palms turned toward to your head, stimulate Bai-Hui with the *qi* ball, as in a massage, but without touching your head. You will feel a light pressure on or tingling sensations in the head.

4. When you feel the *qi* sensations strongly enough, bring the *qi* ball slowly to the back of your head (Nao-Fu), the back of your neck (Da-Chui), Ling-Tai, and to the opposite side of your navel, Ming-Men.

5. Put your hands on the Ming-Men point until it gets warm.

6. Lead the *qi* ball from Xian-Gu to Qi-Hai through Hui-Yin.

7. Bring the *qi* ball from Zhong-Wang, to Tang-Zhong, Tian-Tu, and Yin-Tang, then and back to Bai-Hui.

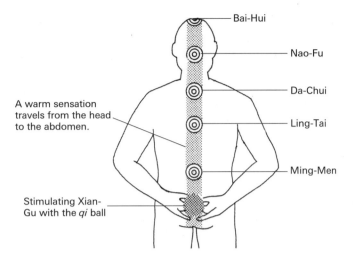

Figure 3–3
The Du (back) Channel of the Microcosmic Orbit method.

A warm sensation travels from the head to the abdomen.

Stimulating Xian-Gu with the *qi* ball

Bai-Hui

Nao-Fu

Da-Chui

Ling-Tai

Ming-Men

General notes on opening the Microcosmic Orbit

1. It is important—in fact absolutely necessary—that the downward meridian is cleared before the upward meridian because *qi* has a tendency to move upward. Particularly when you practice this exercise without an instructor, this step is important in preventing any side effects. To confirm that the meridian is open, pay attention to the sensations you experience. For men, if you feel cool sensations in your head and a warm current flowing from the throat to the lower abdomen along the downward meridian, your downward meridian is open. For women, if you feel cool sensations in your head and a warm current flowing from Da-Chui to Xian-Gu, your downward meridian is open.

2. As *qi* energy from the earth is absorbed from Xian-Gu, stimulate this point well.

3. You will be unable to reach the points between Da-Chui and Ling-Tai with your hands. You just need to imagine that a *qi* ball is being led there, without your hands.

4. Repeat the exercise.

When you finish the exercise, bring a *qi* ball to Qi-Hai, and push the *qi* ball into the lower Dan-Tian. This last step is crucial in preventing any harmful side effects, and so should be borne in mind when you study the *qigong* method on your own. If the *qi* ball is allowed to stay in your head, you may experience numbness or headache, and feel as if you had developed a fever. If you have an abnormally curved cervical vertebra, pain you had there earlier might appear again. If you are a smoker, you might cough or raise some phlegm while a *qi* ball passes by the neck. But do not worry about these symptoms, because they simply show that a *qi* blockage is clearing.

Women's Qi Flows in the Opposite Direction

One day while I was meditating, an idea about the *qi* flow of women flashed into my mind. I suddenly intuited that the direction of women's *qi* flow is opposite that of men.

After mastering the Microcosmic Orbit method, I had begun teaching patients and students to use the *qigong* method I developed to let their *qi* flow smoothly. I found that men achieved satisfactory results, but that women did not. I was not helping to make *qi* flow more smoothly in women. So I followed my intuition and helped women direct their flow of *qi* in the opposite direction.

This worked beautifully. I was quite surprised, since no classical texts mention that *qi* flows in the opposite direction in women. If my hypothesis was correct, I would need to add what I learned to the meridian theory. I needed more objective data. After I stimulated the *qi* flow of the patients in both directions along the Ren and Du channels using magnetism and ultrasound, I tested these patients' *qi* muscle power. Tests of more than one hundred patients made it clear that when *qi* flowed downward along the Du Channel in women (Figure 3–4), the strength of the fingers increased.

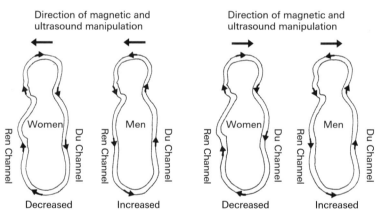

Change in strength of the fingers (as measured with the Reflection of *Qi* Muscle Power test)

Figure 3–4
Difference between flow of *qi* in men and women.

I announced my discovery at the "World *Qigong* Science Conference" in Beijing in 1988, and also published an article on the subject in the professional *qigong* magazine "Zhong Hua *Qigong*." It seems that China, where *qigong* was originally invented, tends to recognize the idea of different directions for the *qi* flow of men and women. I would also note that while this phenomenon is rare, there are men whose *qi* flows in the direction of a woman's, and women whose *qi*-flow direction is the same as most men's. The reason for this is not yet clear.

IV — The Invention of the Cosmic Headband

What Is the Cosmic Headband?

As was mentioned earlier, *qi* flow is affected by the direction of any applied magnetic or ultrasound stimulation. The Reflection of *Qi* Muscle Power test has proved this to be the case. Based on this new concept of the meridians, I invented the Cosmic Headband as a device intended to facilitate mastery of the Microcosmic Orbit method (Figure 4–1).

Figure 4–1
How to wear the Cosmic Headband.

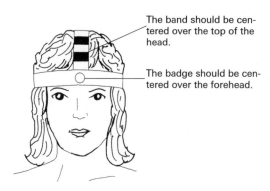

The band should be centered over the top of the head.

The badge should be centered over the forehead.

When you make a *qi* ball between your palms, the Cosmic Headband will help you to experience a sensation of repulsion like that produced by drawing two magnets together, or a tingling sensation akin to electricity and heat, especially as you strengthen the *qi* ball.

I also developed a machine with ultrasound that promotes the Du and Ren channels even more fully than does the Cosmic Headband. I use it clinically to treat patients who suffer from chronic pain. Patients who have never practiced *qigong* can feel *qi* in the upper and lower abdomen. The machine helps to relieve pain more than seventy percent of the time.

For the structure of the Cosmic Headband, I chose, after a great deal of experimentation, special magnetic bars with adequate sizes and strengths. These are set in a row over the center of the head (the Yin-Tang acupuncture point). This magnetizes the area—from the back to front for men, and from the front to back for women.

Here are the facts that I have ascertained about the Cosmic Headband:

1. Its magnetic stimulus can promote *qi* flow, and the human body adjusts in a short time to constant stimulation.

2. The Cosmic Headband and the Reflection of *Qi* Muscle Power test make it possible to know if a particular *qigong* exercise is appropriate for a particular patient.

3. The Cosmic Headband and the Reflection of *Qi* Muscle Power test make it possible to gauge a patient's level.

How to Use the Cosmic Headband

Now you are walking through the unseen world of *qi*. You may sometimes wonder if the path you are on is the right one. Or you might feel uneasy because you are not sure where the path is leading. These worries are natural. But they are also stumbling-blocks that can impede your progress. Figure 4–2 gives you an overview of how you can determine your *qi* ability.

In the visible world, you often know precisely where you stand. For instance, if you are a martial artist, a free fight will tell you who is stronger. If you are a college student, exams and papers constantly offer a standard by which to measure yourself against others. If you are in business, you can point to specific achievements. But in the unseen *qi* world, it has long been impossible to know what you have achieved or at what level you stand.

The Cosmic Headband and the Reflection of *Qi* Muscle Power test offer a way to gauge one's level in the *qi* world. I have given this test to many patients who wore the Cosmic Headband. I found that magnetic stimulation in the opposite direction did not influence patients who had mastered the Microcosmic Orbit. These people were capable of controlling *qi* in the Ren and Du channels with their minds. Their *qi* muscle power was not weakened at all, even when they wore the Cosmic Headband facing in the opposite direction. Even if one has not mastered the Microcosmic Orbit method, after spending only about an hour practicing it, he or she can still get results—that is, they can use the Cosmic Headband in combination with the Reflection of *Qi* Muscle Power test—as a tool for measuring actual *qi* ability.

The Cosmic Headband has not yet been perfected. As was mentioned, the human body adjusts to being constantly stimulated by the electric magnet. Another problem is that we can only stimulate or judge the magnetic field of *qi*. But since ultrasound gives the same result, the invention of the Cosmic Headband is a first step toward the measurement of *qi* ability.

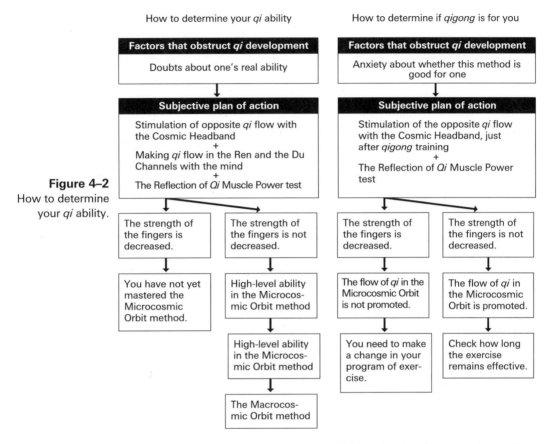

Figure 4–2
How to determine your *qi* ability.

Every method of *qigong* training is unique. This training sheet is meant to be a guide, not a basis for judging anyone else. Please keep in mind that *qigong* is not a competition, but a system for your own growth.

By the way, the Cosmic Headband does not affect people who are full of *qi* energy by nature, or who have a strong *qi* blockage caused by depression or another form of psychological affliction.

In any science, two basic conditions are mandatory: objectivity and independent verification. This is true of the *qi* world as well.

A teacher of mine in Western medicine always said, "What is not yet discovered by scientific knowledge of today will be worth studying as long as it can be measured and replicated. Someday the light of dawn will appear in the darkness."

V — Self-healing Power and Qi

Shamanistic Healing

In this chapter I will explain how the *qigong* method is rooted firmly in the field of medicine.

Early medicine included shamanistic elements that functioned like prayers to comfort and heal the sick. Cultural anthropologists have studied this and reported that even today modern medicine is not the only type of medicine which is used in tribal societies. The works of Carlos Castaneda and Lynn Andrews, for instance, note that the shaman is referred to as a "medicine man," and of his or her having not only shamanistic skills, but also deep knowledge of herbs.

In ancient China, primitive psychic treatments such as Zhu-Yu were common. Yet, even at that time shamanism had its critics. Ci-Ma Qian (145–86? B.C.) wrote that one of the difficulties faced by medical practitioners of the time was people's tendency to "believe shamanism and not believe medicine" in his book "Liu Bu Zhi" (Chinese; "Six difficulties in medical treatment"). In ancient China, shamanistic medicine men and women were placed in charge of medical treatment.

In the *Analects* of Confucius, we read: "Those who do not have stable beliefs are not qualified to become even shamanistic medicine men." This can be interpreted as a form of criticism of shamanistic medical practitioners.

Modern Western medicine attempts to shut out all shamanistic elements. The prevailing attitude in the field is that subjective elements should be excluded from the life sciences, in keeping with the success of the objectivistic study demeanor that has been adopted in physics since Newton. Modern internal medicine is founded on the theory of bacteriology as developed by Pasteur, which holds that infectious disease is caused by bacteria entering a living body. Surgery, on the other hand, is based on the theory that all diseases effect a change in the morbid state of cellular tissue; this theory of cytopathology originated with Virchow (Figure 5–1).

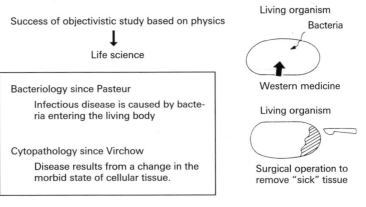

Figure 5–1
View of modern Western medicine.

These two theories are accepted today almost without criticism. If you catch a cold or have a sore throat, you will naturally believe that the bacteria in your body should be killed with antibiotics. If you have a tumor, it must be removed by an operation. These are the most common medical beliefs about diseases. People working in the field of modern medicine—who do not know enough about psychoneuroimmunology—deny the well-established fact that the human immune system is itself an effective basis for medical treatment of many diseases. They prefer to think that diseases disappear if etiological factors are controlled by medicine, and if tumors and the like are cut away. They do not take into consideration the vital force of a living body, because elements such as "vital force" cannot be evaluated objectively, and therefore lie beyond their cognitive ability. The paradigm of "objectivity" is the paradigm not only of medical training but of the whole of academic education in general.

Invisible Qi

Scientists study the world with the basic assumption that any phenomena can be analyzed by breaking them down into smaller and smaller elements.

According to this paradigm, the physical sciences are concerned with analyzing physical phenomena. In biochemistry and related subjects such as molecular biology, biomedical phenomena are analyzed. Psychological phenomena are explained as a function of the physiology of nerves leading to and from the brain (Figure 5–2).

Material phenomena	Physical science
Life phenomena	Life science Biochemistry Biochemistry
Psychological phenomena	The workings of the mind = the functioning of the brain and the neural system.
World view	A philosophy that argues that things can be completely explained by reference to their physical constituents (reductionism).

Figure 5–2
Objective paradigm.

As soon as you go beyond this paradigm, you will encounter opposition. Needless to say, one of the most famous paradigm shifts in history occurred when Copernican theory replaced the Ptolemaic. As you know, Galileo Galilei faced great hardship.

My own "paradigm shift" in medicine occurred when I began to study Chinese medicine and to experience *qi* for myself. I ascertained then that the basic functioning of the human body and the onset of disease cannot be fully explained by Western medicine alone, with its focus on the functioning of the organs, and that the concept of *qi* basic to Chinese medical traditions is absolutely essential to understanding human health and disease (Figure 5–3).

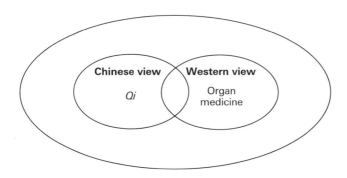

Figure 5–3
An area of overlap in medical "reality."

Let me explain by way of analogy: An automobile is a machine built using the most advanced scientific technology. If something goes wrong with it, you disassemble it, and replace the broken parts. You can understand an automobile as an assemblage composed of all its necessary parts. This is just one example of reductionism.

The situation is quite different, however, when we consider the computer. You will never be able to observe what is involved in its drawing a picture or making a calculation, no matter how completely you disassemble the computer. Even if you use an electron microscope, you will only see circuits of thin lines.

This is because a computer is a totally different machine from any that has existed before. Information is processed by software, which is unseen. Mind, *qi,* or consciousness is like the software of a computer (Figure 5–4). Chinese medicine—including the *qigong* method— could be considered a system of techniques for utilizing the software or information essential to human beings.

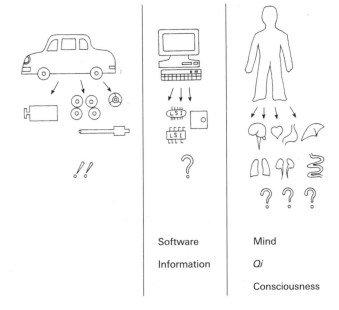

Figure 5–4
Differences among machines, computers, and humans.

Software

Information

Mind

Qi

Consciousness

Combining Qigong with Western Medical Treatment

I would like to explain now what the fact of human *qi* being akin to software or information actually means to human existence and medical treatment. The reason I introduce this subject is because of the sad experiences I have had with some patients with serious diseases who visited me too late. They had put their faith in the claims of unprofessional *qigong* healers who did not know the true meaning of *qi.* These patients were told to stop all their Western medical treatments, and told that they were going to be healed with *qi,* or the laying on of hands, alone. When they finally came back to the hospital seeking treatment, it was too late. This has actually happened several times recently. What's more, some patients are very passive in their attitude toward *qi,* thinking that external *qi* treatment is a complete "remedy." Patients of this type make no effort to promote their own vital force or *qi* power.

The following cases will illustrate. One cancer patient who would have had a chance to survive had he undergone an operation, went to see a healer known for the laying on of hands, and was told that an operation was unnecessary. So he ignored the advice of his doctor and refused to undergo the operation. When he finally came back to the hospital, his cancer had already spread and there was nothing to be done. I was extremely saddened and angry. Another case was that of a patient rendered hemiplegic by a stroke. He went with his wife to China to receive *qi* treatment from a famous *qi* master, which by the way was very expensive. His wife showed me a bogus "certificate" that she had received after taking a course there, which proclaimed her capable of healing others with external *qi*. She did not understand that *qi* was something patients needed to foster in themselves, and that it is important that patients not be dependent on healers. I tried to explain the meaning of *qigong* to her, but the things that she had heard in China had become fixed ideas in her mind, and she didn't want to listen to others. Her "certificate" as a *qi* healer didn't mean a thing because she could not handle, and did not even have a basic understanding of, external *qi*.

Qi does not exist in human beings alone, but in everything. A certificate or license does not transmit *qi* ability. If you are able to use external *qi*, why would you even need recognition from others? Do we need a certificate or license for our thoughts or prayers?

Things can be classified in the current reality in terms of their relative importance. When you begin to do this, you will be able to think well and realize that things which seem to be mutually exclusive actually have their own relative importance and roles (Figure 5–5).

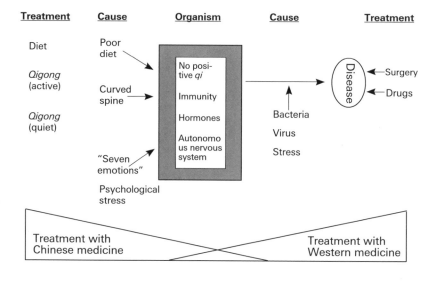

Figure 5–5
The relationship between *qigong* and the development of disease.

Qigong and Western medicine are not meant to be contradictory or mutually exclusive. When the power of *qi* rises in your body, medicines are able to work better, operations can proceed more smoothly, and recovery time can be shortened. I refer to this inclusive, catholic attitude as "mandala thinking." To my mind, every existence has its special significance.

We might well be happier if we could just learn to respond to things by considering—rather than immediately denying—their intrinsic significance.

VI — Qi Training for Mind and Body

Changing the Taste of Food with the Qi Ball

Now you may want to try convincing others of the reality of *qi*. You can show them how the taste of food changes, for a demonstration of the use of *qi* at a physical level. When you make a *qi* ball in keeping with the principles of the Microcosmic Orbit method, you can change the taste of whiskey, wine, cigarettes, or anything that has a strong aroma or flavor.

Experiment using your favorite drink. First, make a concentrated *qi* ball in your palms; your aim will then be to fill the glass with *qi*. Visualize *qi* spiralling into the drink clockwise. Compare the taste or aroma with and without *qi*, and ask others to do the same. You can also check your energy level relative to other people's with the Reflection of Qi Muscle Power test.

It seems that almost anyone can change the taste of food or drink after practicing making a *qi* ball while wearing the Cosmic Headband; the only requirement, though, is that the tester be healthy and eager to succeed. This exercise involves a form of external *qi* that even beginners can handle easily. But if the tester is skeptical or full of doubts, the exercise cannot be expected to succeed, since *qi* activity is intimately linked to the mind and imagination.

In my laboratory, I used a spectrometer to analyze whiskey (Figure 6–1) before and after the addition of *qi*. This device clearly showed a change in the taste after *qi* had been transmitted to the whiskey. You can easily and confidently demonstrate this test to others. However, if you set out to convince people who are closed to the possibility of the reality of *qi*, you may find that you are wasting your time. But don't let this bother you. In the *qi* world, it is necessary to understand that some people will be apprehensive, or even negative. And if you are to succeed in demonstrating *qi* even to such people, it is essential that you maintain a relaxed, casual attitude.

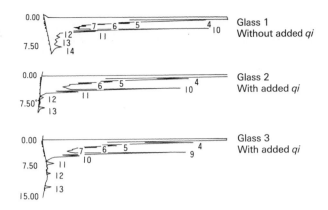

Figure 6–1
Spectral analysis of whiskey as influenced by *qi*.

Spoon Bending

You may have seen performances by people on television demonstrating their ability to bend spoons with the power of the mind alone, or you may have read about it. Why not try it yourself? But be aware that you will need stronger powers of visualization to bend a spoon than you needed to change the taste of food.

Using the Microcosmic Orbit method, gather *qi* energy at an acupuncture point: Shan-Zhong, Jiu-Wei, or Qi-Hai. Alternatively, you can use the Macrocosmic Orbit method, if you have mastered it. Choose whichever of these acupuncture points you prefer. Then, change the *qi* energy into a sensation of heat. (Note: If you wish to gather *qi* using the Macrocosmic Orbit method, your lower body should be the point at which you gather the *qi*.)

Next, visualize this heat "mass" passing through your arms and on to the neck of the spoon. After repeating this step several times, you will feel heat and some softness gather in the neck of the spoon. Next, concentrate *qi* energy into the acupuncture point Yin-Tang (in the middle of your forehead) and look at the spoon from the side, vividly visualizing it as being completely bent. Keep in mind an image of a beam of light streaming from your Yin-Tang, that will bend the spoon. Giving a "command" to the spoon may also help. When you are able to picture the spoon completely bent, pull it lightly with one finger. The spoon will bend like chewing gum, provided that you have vividly pictured this result. There is nothing supernatural about bending a spoon with external *qi*. For that reason, the spoon will not bend by itself, as far as I know, and you will need to pull on it slightly in order to bend it.

Maybe you have heard of people being able to carry extremely heavy objects out of the house during an emergency such as a fire. Bending a spoon is somewhat similar. It is done by activating a hidden power of which you aren't usually aware. In itself, bending a spoon with the power of the mind may sound meaningless, but the point here is simply to have an opportunity to know your hidden power.

To build your confidence, try using a thinner spoon at first. After you succeed with thinner ones, work with spoons that are too thick to bend by force alone.

Recovering from Fatigue

In the Department of Oriental Medicine which is one of the departments under my charge, I invite patients to *qigong* exercise classes when treatment with Chinese herbs alone does not seem to be sufficient.

Patients often tell me, "Once I had learned to do the Microcosmic Orbit method, the fatigue I felt before the exercise was completely gone."

I measured lactic acid, the level of which in the bloodstream is a reliable indicator of fatigue. This involved taking blood samples from patients before and after they had performed the Microcosmic Orbit method. Patients showed a lower level of lactic acid after doing the Microcosmic Orbit method than before (Figure 6–2).

Before: Checked after thirty minutes in a sitting position
After: Checked fifty minutes after the conclusion of *qigong* training

Qigong Level	Patient	Before training	After training	Difference	Patient			
						(Usual level: 3.3–14.9 mg/dl)		
Beginner 3–6 months	A	9.0	11.2	+2.2				
	B	7.7	9.2	+1.5				
	C	8.9	10.5	+1.6				
	D	11.5	5.2	+6.3				
Intermediate 6–12 months	E	17.7	11.6	-6.1	I	6.4	5.0	-1.4
		17.3	9.8	-7.5				
	F	11.2	7.3	-3.9				
	G	6.7	6.0	-0.7				
	H	12.3	10.9	-1.4				
		13.7	9.6	-4.1				
Advanced 7–12 months	J (Chronic hepatitis, irregular pulse (arrhythmia))	9.6	10.8	+1.2	M	9.0	6.6	-2.4
		15.0	9.9	-5.1		9.5	6.0	-3.5
		6.8	8.1	+1.8		11.8	6.5	-5.5
	K (Chronic hepatitis, gout)	8.6	9.7	-1.1	N	8.0	3.1	-4.9
		13.8	9.7	-4.1		12.3	12.4	+0.1
		7.4	7.0	-0.4		9.5	9.4	-0.1
	L	11.0	8.4	-2.6	O (Asthma)	8.9	8.9	0.0
		9.1	8.6	-0.5		8.7	10.4	+1.7
		9.9	8.4	-1.5		7.9	7.3	-0.6

Figure 6–2
Changes in the lactic acid level of the blood serum after *qigong* training.

From the perspective of kinetic physiology, this is a very interesting result. Usually, movement causes an increase in the amount of lactic acid in the bloodstream, but the Microcosmic Orbit method instead caused a decrease. The amount of lactic acid in many samples was even lower than that seen in people who had been at rest for half an hour.

People seem to recover from ordinary fatigue through the performance of the Microcosmic Orbit method. I also measured patients' blood pressure before and after *qigong* exercise. I found that high blood pressure decreased, and that blood pressure that was too low, rose. *Qigong* exercise helps to return blood pressure to optimal levels (Figure 6–3). These experiments show that *qigong* can rightly be thought of as an active form of rest.

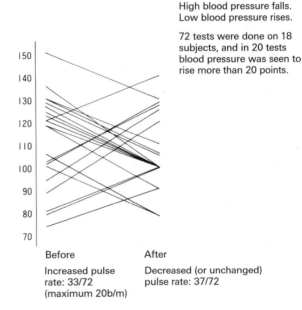

Figure 6–3 Normalization of blood pressure after *qigong* exercise.

High blood pressure falls.
Low blood pressure rises.

72 tests were done on 18 subjects, and in 20 tests blood pressure was seen to rise more than 20 points.

Before

Increased pulse rate: 33/72 (maximum 20b/m)

After

Decreased (or unchanged) pulse rate: 37/72

The *qigong* exercise that I am referring to here is the Microcosmic Orbit method, not the advanced training usually done by practitioners of the martial arts. If you are practicing *qigong* alone while watching training videos, for instance, remember that feeling comfortable and relaxed is one of the most important points in *qigong* training.

I am not presuming to say that the results of just these two tests involving the metabolic system (lactic acid) and the circulatory system (blood pressure) completely prove the efficacy of the *qigong* method. However, the results of these experiments do begin to prove that the Microcosmic Orbit method is a means by which a student can raise his or her own energy level. Given the rapid greying of our society, there is no doubt that we need to continue our scientific research into the benefits of the *qigong* method.

Patients and Qigong

Qigong exercise can help patients to make not only physical but also psychological gains. One of my patients, who is forty-five years old, suffers from chronic hepatitis and gout (see Figure 6–2). He has been practicing *qigong* in my class for two years. He reports that, "I don't worry about my physical condition so much any more, and I am less bothered by negative results of a particular checkup than I was before. I feel so much better after *qigong* exercise. I have less soreness in my shoulders. Circulating *qi* through my body makes me more aware of my body in subtle ways. I feel thankful for the organs that allow me to live. As for the relationships with my colleagues at work, I think I have gotten more generous with them. I don't get angry so easily, and I'm able to forgive. I can respect the situation of others more than before. In business meetings, I used to insist on my opinions, but now I listen to others first. As a result, people accept my opinion more often now. For the first time, I realize that I'm the only one who can cure my illness. These days, I am confident that I can remain unaffected by problems, and deal with them as they arise. I have started to know myself better now."

The essence of *qigong* is extracted from the mental and physical culture of the Far East. It is not a religion, and it has no doctrine. In my *qigong* class, I taught this student just the *qigong* exercise from the Microcosmic Orbit method. However, he also learned how to heal himself, and learned some of the ways in which *qi* affects relationships.

His evaluation encouraged me. At the time, I was much too quick to put things into words than I am now. I often advised patients to be thankful for their bodies, to respect the situation of others, to be slow to anger, and to try to cure their illness themselves. These things were easy enough for me to say, but much harder for patients to do. I worried about talking to them too much, because I did not want patients to get the impression that I was preaching, or that I was interested in passing on to them any sort of doctrine.

Many other patients also wrote descriptions that carefully traced changes in their awareness. As I had been interested in psychosomatics since my days in medical school, I understood that illness resulted more or less from both physical and mental factors, but I was not sure just how to create an effective method that would address both sides at once. My patients provided me critical information for achieving exactly this—a natural way to increase awareness through *qigong* exercises. This was a great help to my *qigong* study. That's why I say my patients are my actual teachers in the *qigong* method.

VII — Kinesiology

The Role of the Reflection of Qi Muscle Power Test

In order to be convinced of the validity of the Reflection of *Qi* Muscle Power test, you will need to repeat the test many times. A hundred tests with consistent results may be enough to make a tester or patient accept the test's validity, so try performing the test ten times a day for ten days. But do also take the following points into consideration:

1. Team up with a healthy person who has a positive attitude.
2. The patient should remove any metallic accessories like rings, watches, necklaces, or magnets.
3. Avoid locations near electrical appliances. These appliances produce strong electromagnetic waves which can weaken finger power and alter test results.
4. Tester and patient should both perform the test without prejudice, and without speculating on the outcome.

Over the years I have tested countless objects, and particularly food, in an effort to uncover the meaning of "*qi* muscle reflection." For testing I have usually chosen a certain kind of food, and then tested various examples of this food, of varying quality. After performing the test, I always checked the taste as well. I found that the poorer the food's quality, the more finger power was reduced. I even had difficulty swallowing the food of the lowest quality. This suggested to me that when food was of very poor quality, the throat muscle, which is supposed to aid in swallowing, did not work properly. Such experiments helped me to better understand the reflection of *qi* muscle power.

Survival is the primary instinct not only of humans but of all living creatures. Modern life does not usually present us with constant threats to our survival, but certainly in past ages humans needed constantly to be concerned about extremely practical matters, and in certain parts of the globe this is still true. In former ages, every choice, no matter how small it might seem, was a matter of survival. Is an object edible, or inedible? Is it potable? Is this spot safe to settle in? Is that person a friend or an enemy? ... and so on. One mistake could be deadly. Under conditions like that, correct judgments about the body were necessary for a person's very survival. I believe that this ability is instinctual, and that *qi* muscle reflection is based on instinctual abilities of this sort.

Even if we rarely use this ability, it is a part of our genes, since we are the descendants of primitive man.

Here is a test that might be interesting to try.

Boil water in two ways: in a kettle over an open flame, and in a cup in a microwave oven. Then pour the water into two identical cups. When the water has cooled enough to handle, place your hand above each cup, put your fingertips into it, and then try performing the Reflection of *Qi* Muscle Power test.

The clarity and sharpness of the results may surprise you. Water heated in a microwave oven considerably reduces the power of the fingers. In my experience, when I have performed this test, finger power was reduced in about seventy of every hundred patients who were unfamiliar with the Reflection of *Qi* Muscle Power test. When I performed the test on people who were already familiar with it, this reduction was seen in all patients. In both cases, after performing the test, I asked patients to slowly drink the water. Thirty out of a hundred people who were new to the test said that water heated in the microwave was difficult to swallow, and that they were, on the other hand, easily able to drink water that had been heated in the kettle.

Water has a dynamic order with vibrating H_2O molecules. The structure of the vibration of water can be compared to synchronized swimming. When water is treated in the microwave oven, the violent vibration of the electromagnetic waves destroy the dynamic order. Such drinking water does not exist in nature. And humans do have the ability to sense this distinction.

The Future of the Reflection of Qi Muscle Power Test

In the future, when our society recognizes the Reflection of *Qi* Muscle Power test, we may see a paradigm shift. At that point, people might very well begin to assess the value of health food, medicine, or even ordinary foods on the basis of *qi* energy. Exaggerated claims in advertising will no longer be acceptable. Pesticidal traces or additives in food will be easy to spot. Experts in this test who also have medical training will be able to perform cancer screenings and to help detect cancer in its early stages. It is imperative that we continue to conduct rigorous research into this test.

When a tester performs this test, most patients who have never experienced the test before have some doubt that his or her strength is actually being controlled simply by the tester's pulling on the fingers. But after trying the test several times, patients usually notice a change in their own strength. Yet there are always some who remain unconvinced. If we had a machine we could use to measure the strength of our fingers ourselves, we might be more readily convinced. Someday someone will invent such a machine.

VIII — All Things Have Vibration

The Self Reflection of Qi Muscle Power Test

The Reflection of *Qi* Muscle Power test can also be performed alone. I discovered this possibility quite by accident. One day, a tester was about to perform the test on me, and I noticed a change in the strength of my fingers even before he touched my hands.

When you master the following Self Reflection of *Qi* Muscle Power test, you can ascertain whether an object has positive or negative *qi* energy.

1. Form a ring with the thumb and the index finger of your right hand, and apply strength to it. Feel the pressure of your fingers and of the muscles of your arm.

2. With your left hand, touch the object that you want to check, imagining that you are inhailing *qi* from it. You can check any object this way, such as food, drink, medicine, etc.

3. If the object's *qi* is positive for you, you will be able to maintain the strength in the ring and in your arm. If it is negative, the strength will leave both the ring and your arm. For instance, try it with a cigarette in your left hand, to experience the decreased strength of the ring.

However, you need to be sensitive enough to feel subtle changes in your muscles, and you need to have a positive attitude. You must also have a desire to master the Reflection of *Qi* Muscle Power test. If you assume that it cannot work, then unfortunately the test will not. Before you try the test by yourself, increase your confidence by doing the standard Reflection of *Qi* Muscle Power test with someone else.

Enjoy the test with your friends. Learning from someone else is usually the fastest way to learn. Once you master this test, you will be sure of the reality and the nature of *qi*. Try this test whenever and wherever you are. It will help increase your sensitivity to *qi*. You can use it with foods to learn with certainly what you should and shouldn't eat. Checking a cigarette with the Reflection of *Qi* Muscle Power test is likely to make you want to quit. Checking medicines, however, is not always reliable, since some medicines have the intended effect only on certain internal organs or infected areas, and could do harm if applied to the entire body.

Take the Reflection of *Qi* Muscle Power test for fun and exchange opinions with your *qi* friends. If there is consensus among you, it can be said that you understand *qi* quite well. (For further information, see also Chapter XVIII, the section on "The *Qi* Consensus Method.")

Dowsing

The principles involved in dowsing are not totally clear, but dowsing is now recognized as a replicable procedure. Dowsing is a method of catching vibrations with radiesthesia, using a tool such as the pendulum or the L-rod. During the course of my own work with dowsing, I learned that a pendulm or an L-rod magnifies minute movements of or subtle changes in the muscles. If you have an opportunity to try this procedure, use a pendulum with a fixed fulcrum or an L-rod with the handgrips fixed.

"Hand-dowsing" refers to radiesthesia without the use of any special tools. If you practice hand-dowsing, you will be able to use your fingers as antenna for *qi*.

How to perform hand-dowsing

1. Spread the fingers of one hand. Visualize an area the size of a ping-pong ball between your thumb and index finger.
2. Rub the imaginary ball gently with two fingers and you will feel a *qi* ball.
3. Do the same with the other fingers and make four *qi* balls between the fingers of your right hand.
4. Touch your little finger with your thumb, then release. Repeat this. This will allow you to make a *qi* ball on the Lao-Gong acupuncture point (at the center of your palm).
5. When you are able to feel all five *qi* balls distinctly, gather them together into a single *qi* ball in your palm (Figure 8–1).

Now place your hand over the object to be checked, inhale *qi* from it, and feel the changes to the *qi* ball in your hand. This is hand-dowsing.

If you continue this training, your hand will become very sensitive. Imagine that your *qi* and tactual senses develop in concert and that your tactual sense is now increasing. Your palm will start to work like the tactual organ of an insect. Interestingly enough, when you can easily make a good *qi* ball in your hand, your fingers may move unconsciously.

Make *qi* balls between your fingers and on the Lao-Gong acupuncture point.

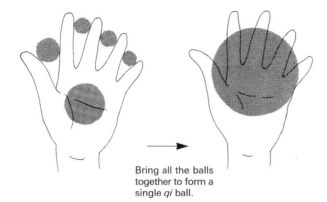

Bring all the balls together to form a single *qi* ball.

Figure 8–1
Make a *qi* ball with one hand.

The Reflection of *Qi* Muscle Power test and dowsing are both ways of recognizing the vibrations of *qi* through changes in or subtle movement of muscles which a human being receives subconsciously.

Hand-dowsing can be explained as a method to recognize the vibration of *qi* in connection with the tactual sense. However, it is not yet possible to measure the energy of *qi* mechanically, so we are capable only of measuring its effect.

The sense of *qi* attained by hand-dowsing has a delicate nuance and is too subtle to describe in words. Expect to enjoy this exercise, and to feel the sensations gradually. For instance, if an object's *qi* is positive for you, you will feel soft sensations and sense minute vibrations. If its *qi* is negative, you will sense hard, rough vibrations, and cold or strained sensations (Figure 8–2).

Keep practicing until you can easily and immediately make a *qi* ball in either hand. This ability makes it possible to learn the techniques of checking an abnormally curved backbone or the *qi* flow of the Microcosmic Orbit.

Positive and Negative Qi and Breathing

If at some time you are unable to do hand-dowsing because an object cannot be touched, try the following steps.

Figure 8–2 Effects of positive and negative *qi*.

	Muscle strength	Muscle flexibility	Veins	Pain	Breathing	Blood flow	Concentration	Taste	Plants
Positive *qi*	Increases	Increases	Expand	Decreases	Is easier	Increases	Is enhanced	Is milder	Grow
Negative *qi*	Decreases	Decreases	Contract	Increases	Is more difficult	Decrease	Weakens	Is rather unpleasant	Stop growing

1. Relax and breathe normally several times, paying particular attention to your inhalation.

2. Become aware of the third eye, or Ying-Tang. Look at the object that you want to check, and imagine that you are inhaling its *qi*.

3. If you feel that you are able to inhale deeply, down to the bottom of your stomach, you should consider the object's *qi* to be positive. On the contrary, if you feel that you are unable to inhale deeply, as if you were being choked, the object's *qi* is negative for you.

Practice this method step by step, using paintings, pictures, people, and places, as you like. Soon you will begin to enjoy some success. For instance, when you are at a sushi bar, you can choose pieces of fresh fish that have the highest amounts of *qi* energy, by using this breathing method. This is a good way to remind yourself of its effectiveness. I enjoy doing this with my *qi* friends. Interestingly, everybody chooses the same kind of fish most of the time. (The only drawback is the bill—you are likely to choose the freshest pieces, and these can be pricey!)

Checking a person's *qi* is not so easy because a person's emotional state and overall condition fluctuate constantly, and their feelings toward you also matter. If we think of the old saying "like attracts like" for a moment as a *qi* phenomenon, people whose vibrations fit well together can "breathe" together naturally, and such people tend to gravitate unconsciously toward one another. It's also true that something that has positive energy for you may have negative energy for someone else.

Receiving Good Luck

Are you a lively person who thinks positively? Are you a lucky person? If you are cheerful by nature, others will want to be with you. They'll sense that they tend to receive good luck through you and that they can feel comfortable around you even without conversation. The reverse holds true as well. If you are a gloomy person characterized by negative thinking and bad luck, others will feel constrained and stay away.

Though we don't usually think seriously about these matters, we are influenced by the flow of *qi* whenever we communicate or align ourselves with others. This is why I would suggest that you maximize your contact with people who are cheerful and lucky, while making an effort to become such a person yourself.

These days, an increasing number of people are practicing all kinds of exercises, including *qigong*. Some develop a sensitivity to *qi*, and then gradually attain a deep understanding of other people's suffering. Since they align themselves with the suffering and guilt of others, at times they become gloomy themselves. In order to prevent this, it is important to remember that human beings are meant to live freely and pleasantly. Being congnizant of the principles of freedom and pleasure is one of the most important things a *qi* trainee can do. If trainees overlook this important principle, training in *qigong* can have negative effects, such as depression or feelings of emptiness. If trainees must associate with people who attract bad luck or whose *qi* energy is weak, they should wait until they have mastered the way to absorb external *qi* from the earth and space through the Macrocosmic Orbit method.

Qi and Antiques

For people who have a well-developed sense of *qi*, an antique exhibition can be an interesting place to spend some time. Once I visited an antique show displaying all kinds of items from around the world. As soon as I entered the room, I felt that the air was thick and whirling with a mixture of positive and negative *qi*. Obviously, every item was radiating its own *qi*, and the combination was making the atmosphere very strange. I told the dealer that I could judge if an item was real or fake, with my intuition alone. We looked around together. She was interested in testing how accurate my judgment really was.

First of all, we stood before an old image of Buddha, which was radiating a soft and subtle warmth. I told her that it must be real. She told me that it had been appraised as a real antique by a connoisseur. There was an image of an ancient Chinese soldier radiating a rough and cold *qi*. This apparently was an old guardian soldier that had been used to decorate a grave in China. Some items that looked very valuable radiated no *qi*. I felt good *qi* emanating from some items that looked simple and primitive. For example, one vessel gave me a peaceful impression and I felt comfortable looking at it. I found out that it had been used for a long time as a container for Buddhist scriptures. A mask of a pharaoh from Egypt, on the other hand, was horrible. Its *qi* was like a crouching black mass. When I told her that the piece had an extremely negative *qi* although it was a real antique, she agreed and said that looking at it always gave her a headache. My judgment at the exhibition was successful. The manager and I had the same opinion on nearly every item. However, I must confess that there were also some fake antiques at the show from which I received very good *qi* energy.

IX — Simple Tools for Qi Control

Goods for Conscious Energy

You may have seen all kinds of talismans advertised in alternative health magazines—pyramids, crystals, power seals, and so forth. Friends and acquaintances often bring me talismans and tools. Some people bring these to me and ask me to check their energetic effect. There are talismans or tools on the market that actually do release high-quality *qi* energy. But many, instead, are simply far too expensive and, what's worse, don't release much *qi*. They are advertised as talismans that will bring you luck and health if you wear them on your body. However, most are not supportive tools for *qi* training. On the other hand, if they help people to become more aware of the *qi* world, I won't say that buying such talismans is always bad.

The vajras I have made are of three different kinds: single, three-pronged, and five-pronged. All are made of fine ceramics, and are certain to be useful as supportive tools for anyone who wishes to learn to control *qi* energy. When a trainee has learned to control external *qi*, he or she is advised to try to learn to manage the esoteric power from space, by means of the power of visualization and their firm belief. Learning to do this as well will allow a trainee to release the same vibrations as are given off by the supportive vajra tools. Trainees should use these tools simply to reach higher levels, and stop using them when they are no longer needed.

A Qi Tool You Can Make Yourself

Do you find it difficult, despite your regular practice of the Microcosmic Orbit method, to make a *qi* ball? Quite often, people ask me to recommend some effective and inexpensive supportive tool to help them succeed in this basic exercise. That was why I invented the Vital

Ball. It's easy and inexpensive to make, and it releases *qi* of quite high quality. It stands up in comparison to many of the better supportive tools now on the market.

If you have not succeeded in sensing *qi* yet, try this: Hold the Vital Ball in both hands and bend over, bringing your head toward your knees. Isn't your body more flexible with it than without it? Perform the Reflection of *Qi* Muscle Power test, or observe your breathing. Isn't your breathing smoother with the Vital Ball? If your shoulders were stiff before, no doubt they feel better after the exercise. If you are able to control *qi* energy, rotate the Vital Ball clockwise above a drink or an item of food. You can use the Vital Ball to change the taste of food this way. It can heal pain too. Just turn it clockwise over the painful part of the body. If you are already able to sense *qi* well, try performing the Microcosmic Orbit method while holding the Vital Ball. Your movement and the flow of your *qi* will be smoother than before.

Try meditating with six Vital Balls placed around you in a hexagonal shape, and you will be able to reach a deep stage right away (Figure 9–1). You might even become addicted to this method. If you are curious and have time, increase the number of Vital Balls used in your meditation, or change their shape from a circle to a cone or pyramid. Although I invented this for humans, it may be able to improve the efficiency of combustion engines as well.

Figure 9–1
Meditation with Vital Balls.

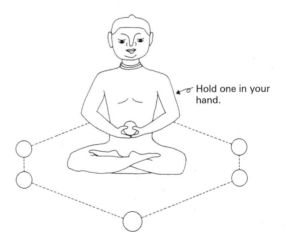

Hold one in your hand.

Place the Vital Balls around you in a hexagonal shape. Hold one in your hand.

How does the Vital Ball produce *qi* energy? According to the results of my research, cosmic energy or *qi* energy can be utilized when physical energy, form energy, material energy, and conscious energy are combined. The Vital Ball works on the principle that all creatures have properties of vibration.

The Vital Ball is made of copper wire, tissue paper, and aluminum foil. The tissue paper serves to separate the copper wire and aluminum foil. I suppose that copper and aluminum (physical energy) resonate in addition to the spiral energy (form energy), and that space energy is produced. You may wonder why I used copper and aluminum as my materials. I experimented with these materials after learning that independent space energy researcher Kenji Abe had discovered that the vibrations produced by the combination of copper and aluminum resonate particularly well together. There may still be other metal combinations that would produce space energy through the resonance of their vibrations. Further research is warranted.

The Four Elements of Space Energy

As we will see later, in Chapters XII and XVII, vacuums are not actually composed of empty space; they are full of positive and negative energy—in other words, conscious energy, or the energy of prana. Limitless energy can be produced from space. Form energy, material energy, and conscious energy are subjects considered today to be outside the purview of science. But when the usefulness of space energy—that is, free energy—to industry is recognized, these three forms of energy will come to be viewed as basic elements. Then physical energy such as the already popular electromagnetic power, will be combined with various materials, and techniques for obtaining energy from space will be invented.

Space energy has four main elements, each taking many forms (Figure 9–2):

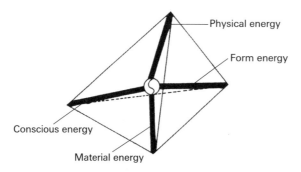

Physical energy

Form energy

Conscious energy

Material energy

Figure 9–2
The four main elements of space energy.

The trigonal pyramid with four elements determines the quality and quantity of space energy.

1. Form energy: pyramids, *taiji* diagrams with intertwined yin and yang, unique hexagonal shapes known as *hilanya*, regular polyhedronical structures such as the regular tetrahedron or regular octahedron, coils, fractal structures, Möbius bands, Klein bottles, the golden section, etc.

2. Material energy: fine ceramics (for example, the energy of zirconium suits the human body well), jewels, gemstones, things that have a uniform crystal structure, things treated with intense heat, combinations of different metals, things that have absorbed space energy for a long time or in large amounts (for instance, water absorbs *qi* energy well), and combinations of colors.

3. Conscious energy: We can release conscious energy by means of visualization and firm belief.

4. Physical energy: Energy such as electromagnetic power; this includes electric currents in coils, spark discharges, resonance circuits, ultrasound waves, etc.

There are many more forms of energy, and in fact I would need to write several books if I wanted to do justice to this one subject. Unfortunately it is still difficult to research either cosmic energy or free energy today, since no conventional machinery exists that is capable of measuring them.

I used my intuition and sensitivity to *qi* to invent the Vital Ball, which is a combination of form energy and material energy. In order to develop techniques for using space energy in the future, a combination of marked sensitivity to *qi* and great familiarity with the latest scientific techniques will be necessary.

The twenty-first century will be an era of space energy or *qi* energy. In preparation for this new era, I have systematized the Microcosmic Orbit method and the Macrocosmic Orbit method so that we will be able to accept them simply on the basis of our common sense. There is no reason why you cannot also invent generators of space energy, using form energy, material energy, conscious energy, and physical energy combined with your own intuition and sensitivity to *qi*. At the same time, you will want to try to open the Chakras, since we can receive space energy through them; practice the Macrocosmic Orbit method to do this.

Whenever you use talismans, you should make an effort to understand as clearly as possible their significance and what they represent. And of course you should remember that your aim is to eventually use *qi* energy from space without any special tools.

Finally, I would just note that the Vital Ball can cause a temporary change in the state of your health, because of the strength with which it releases *qi* energy. Beginners should avoid using the Vital Ball intensively.

How to Make a Vital Ball

You will need: aluminum foil, copper wire (between a half and one millimeter in diameter; the thinner, the better) tissue paper (Figure 9–3).

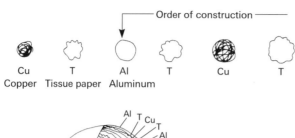

When it is six or seven layers thick, the Vital Ball will be about the size of a softball.

Remember to use the thinnest possible copper wires.

Figure 9–3
Making a Vital Ball.

1. Roll the copper wire into a ball the size of a ping-pong ball.

2. Wrap the ball twice in tissue paper.

3. Wrap it once in aluminum foil.

4. Wrap it in tissue paper again.

5. Roll it with copper wire as tightly as possible.

6. Wrap it with tissue paper again.

7. Repeat steps 3 through 5 six or seven times, or until the ball is about ten centimeters in diameter.

PART TWO

Healing Others

X — The Macrocosmic Orbit Method

Healing Patients

Now that you have mastered the Microcosmic Orbit method, you probably feel refreshed after *qigong* training and have learned to release *qi* from your hands. In China, *qi* researchers have documented that infrared rays and magnetic energy are released from the hands. An increase of infrared rays was also seen in my research. This supports the theory that the essence of *qi* is infrared rays, or magnetic energy. *Qigong* practitioners actually treat patients in hospitals in China.

Once one can release *qi* from the hands, it becomes possible to heal patients. I practice *qi* healing with various patients who come for treatment to my department. Some patients enjoy great benefits from this method. It is common for patients who complain of pain in their muscles or bones to be healed after just one or two sessions; I sometimes find acupuncture treatments to be very successful as well. I find that the results are usually better when I include some form of gentle manipulation of *qi* in my treatment.

In the early years, though, one problem soon arose: even though *qi* healing was interesting and I was happy to be able to practice it, I noticed that I was becoming exhausted. What was worse, I began to show the same symptoms as my patients. I was able to get rid of my exhaustion by performing the Microcosmic Orbit method; but as soon as I had treated a patient, for instance, who complained of chronic stiffness in the shoulders, my own shoulders started aching. After I had seen someone who had a stomachache, my own stomach began to hurt. This was happening too often to interpret as mere synchronicity. For a while I had no idea what to do. From my many years of training in the martial arts, I could understand that I needed to accept difficulties of this sort as a natural part of the road to progress, because I knew that my symptoms were caused by something that had to do with the method that I was using to handle external *qi*. In fact, I almost wanted to give up *qi* healing altogether, because of these symptoms and my exhaustion. But there were patients waiting for me, whom I was actually able to help with *qi* healing. There seemed to be no way to return to the point where I knew nothing about *qi*. During this period, I read all sorts of documents in an effort to find some way beyond my own limitations. After a long process of trial and error, I finally realized how important the mind and consciousness were to *qi* healing.

Healing and the Development of the Mind

If you have practiced martial arts seriously over a long period of time, you will notice precisely the moment at which you finally progress to a higher level. And any improvement will bring joy and increased self-confidence. But sooner or later you will discover that there are always people who are at much higher levels than you. This may not prevent you from enjoying the feeling of achievement. I know that thinking about the significance of healing lessened my exhaustion. But somehow I also always knew that my healing power was not completely natural. When I mastered the Macrocosmic Orbit method, I finally comprehended why I had been so exhausted before. External *qi* released through my Microcosmic Orbit was making me exhausted, because it was like discharging my own electric power. Certainly it is possible to release a strong healing energy with training in the Microcosmic Orbit method, but there is a limit. When you reach this limit, you will feel a lack of *qi* and become exhausted. If, however, your *qi* comes from the Macrocosmic Orbit method, you will not feel a lack of *qi*, because you are simply allowing external *qi* to pass through you. On the contrary, with this method, you will feel a sense of exaltation.

The theory and practice of the Macrocosmic Orbit method are the main theme of this book. My primary aim in writing this is to let you know that your mind can go above the physical level, reach the *qi* level, develop further to the level of soul, and finally go even beyond—namely, to the point of oneness with the universe (Figure 10–1).

In *qigong*, you will let *qi* flow with the Micro/Macrocosmic Orbit methods, which refer to the opening of Chakras, to borrow a term from Yoga. This method has in the past been kept a secret by the handful of people who had so-called paranormal abilities. But nowadays it is no longer a secret. Many different methods are being studied in various parts of the world today in order to absorb the limitless energy from space or earth, including a method for reaching a superconscious state in meditation. *Qigong* is not only a method of improving physical health but also of developing the mind.

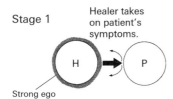

Stage 1

Healer takes on patient's symptoms.

Strong ego

The healer has an attitude of superiority. There is some quantity of *qi*, but the quality is low. Only limited *qi* enters the patient, and it does not make the patient feel comfortable.

Stage 2

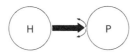

The healer does not have an attitude of superiority, but he is using only his own power. The quality of qi is not high, either. The healer takes on the patient's syptoms, and tires easily.

Stage 3

There is a sense of oneness between the healer and patient, like that between a mother and baby. The quality of *qi* is better. The healer does not take on the patient's symptoms, but still tires easily.

Stage 4

The healer realizes that he or she has the patient's trust. The healer is grateful for the opportunity for self-improvement that comes from healing others. The quality of *qi* is good. The healer does not take on the patient's symptoms, but still tires somewhat.

Stage 5

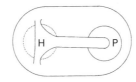

The healer's ego is not important. The healer is tapped into limitless *qi* from space, and heals with external *qi,* without thinking about anything. The healer does not tire, and remains aware that both healer and patient are but a drop in the ocean of *qi*.

Figure 10–1
Stages in the power to heal with *qi*.

Mastering the Macrocosmic Orbit Method

Mastering the Microcosmic Orbit method was for me the first step in beginning to sense and control *qi*. The next step was to master the Macrocosmic Orbit method, and so I spent a good deal of time and effort attempting to absorb external *qi* from nature. I remember the very moment that I succeeded. I had a strong feeling of *qi* on the crown of my head. I felt as if something was rising through my head with a pulsing sensation. Since then I have been able to sense external *qi* and to allow *qi* to flow from space through my body as I wish. As soon as I began to absorb *qi* through the acupuncture point known as Xian-Gu from earth, I began to feel minute vibrations at that point. Since that time, I have never run short of *qi*, and this has allowed me to heal patients without becoming exhausted. When I succeeded in absorbing and releasing external *qi* through my hands, I felt true joy.

Once you begin to absorb external *qi*, you don't need to try to let *qi* flow around your Microcosmic Orbit, because *qi* will flow through your body naturally. Even if you wear the Cosmic Headband the wrong way or hold a bottle of poison in your hand during the Reflection of *Qi* Muscle Power test, these things will have no effect. When you master the Macrocosmic Orbit method, you strengthen the energy field of your body enough to intercept negative energy from the outer world. For example, one of my colleagues, with whom I used to practice *qigong*, had always suffered from a fear of crowds, but as soon as he mastered the Macrocosmic Orbit method, this problem disappeared. The energy field surrounding our bodies can be strengthened tremendously with the Macrocosmic Orbit method. It took me a long time to clarify and systematize the inner workings of the Macrocosmic Orbit method. But I am convinced that this method now consists of useful and practical exercises from which anyone can benefit.

Mastering the Macrocosmic Orbit method requires that we use techniques that are rather advanced, and that several conditions be met. First of all, we must be capable of absorbing the *qi* energy that exists in the celestial sphere, on earth, and in space. Our "channels" for absorbing *qi* energy must be open and functioning properly. We must be able to turn on the "channels" and have practical techniques that we can use to activate them.

XI — Three Chinese Masters and Limitless Qi

Does External Qi Diminish When It Is Released?

Qigong can be divided into two schools: one concentrates on one's own health and the other on healing other people by releasing *qi* energy, or external *qi*.

I of course tend to focus on the healing potential of *qi*. But a well-known teacher of the first school, Master Jiao Guo-Rui, advocates the *qigong* method solely as a means of promoting one's own increased vitality. While this master avoids making any particular statements about releasing external *qi*, he seemed, when I attended a lecture he gave in Japan, to have a somewhat negative opinion of this process. At the same time, I got the impression that he had studied *qigong* quite creatively. I intuited that he would be able to handle external *qi* far better than most ordinary *qigong* practicioners, and I wondered why a master like him would wish to deny the possibility of healing with external *qi*.

And yet when I later observed the methods used by practitioners who sought to heal with external *qi*, and recalled his lecture, I thought I understood what he meant. These *qi* practitioners were more or less dominating their patients. They were sending *qi* rather one-sidedly, and patients did not expect their self-healing power to be activated, but rather tended to depend outright on the *qi* practitioners. This, it seemed, was why Master Jiao Guo-Rui had spoken against "occult" or superstitious *qi*, in which patients thought in terms of an "outside force" beyond their own control, and in which they neglected the true value of self-healing with *qi* energy. This amazing *qigong* master instead wanted to emphasize the power of self-healing.

Qi practitioners remain divided on the question of whether one's own *qi* is diminished by the release of external *qi*. Some say that it is, while others insist that it is possible to absorb limitless quantities of *qi* from earth and space while releasing *qi*.

Master Lin Hou-Shen is one of the most famous masters who argues that *qi* diminishes. He introduced *qigong* anesthesia to the world. I attended a seminar of his in 1987, where he emphasized that we should not release *qi*. According to him, *qi* needs to be recharged in our body by means of training, and it is like a battery in that it runs down with continued use. When he suggested that releasing *qi* posed something like a danger to the practitioner's health, I was very disappointed. I had just mastered the Macrocosmic Orbit method by opening my Chakras, after struggling for a long time at the level of the Microcosmic Orbit, and was disheartened to hear that this progress would now leave me with diminishing *qi*. Friends who had joined me in attending the seminar were also disappointed to hear the viewpoint of Master Lin. I had asked them to come along, telling them that this would be a rare opportunity to meet a great Chinese master.

Then I decided to prove this master wrong, and to show that *qi* would not diminish.

Transcendent Qigong

The AMI machine is capable of measuring meridians electrically. I invented this machine to prove that external *qi* is not diminished by being released. Yet I still also hoped to find a master who would say that our external *qi* is not diminished when we release *qi*. Meanwhile I continued my own training and research, in an effort to improve my own external *qi* ability.

In autumn 1989 I was in Peking to attend the first international *Qigong* Science Council. My presentation was titled "The Different *Qi* Flow in Men and Women." My theme caught people's attention, and the paper was published in the magazine "Zhong-Hua [Chinese] *Qigong*."

An encounter with the unparalleled master Zhao Guang was the most memorable incident in my own development. Our Japanese group visited the *qigong* department of Xi-Yuan Hospital. I was communicating with Master Zhao Guang by writing down Chinese characters which we Japanese were unable to pronounce in Chinese, but the meaning of which we understood, since these same characters are used in our language. I asked him what he thought of the Microcosmic and Macrocosmic Orbit methods. He glanced at me with a smile, then wrote down that he did not practice these methods. I was very confused. He seemed completely unconcerned about the Macrocosmic Orbit! Next I asked him to sense my *qi*. I gripped his hand and used my full power to send him external *qi* through the Macrocosmic Orbit method. He smiled and again wrote something down. The note said, "I don't feel anything."

Isn't this the man they call the "master of masters"? It was so strange, I thought. I finally remembered to turn on the "*qi* computer" in my brain to try to sense the extent of his *qi* power. What I "saw" was, to my surprise, an unbelievable flow of *qi* through him. *Qi* was blowing up from the top of his head, forming an inverse triangle and at the same time it was also flowing into him. In addition, a tremendous amount of *qi* was flowing in and out through the acupuncture point Xian-Gu, in the shape of a pyramid. Even though I sent him *qi*, it went straight through him, as if his body was transparent. When I tried to receive *qi* from him, it rushed toward me like a huge wave. The whole time I was trying all these things, he just stood there smiling as if nothing was happening. When I closed my eyes, his very molecules seemed to have dissipated through the air; it seemed as if he was not there. Even when he was standing there in a quite ordinary way, he was releasing strong and wonderful *qi* that appeared limitless.

Suddenly the meaning of his words flashed into my mind, and I intuited that what he meant was: *You seem to know what the Macrocosmic Orbit is, but you still have a long way to go, because you rely on your power. You must understand that there is a stage in which one himself becomes the Macrocosmic Orbit.* His phrase, "I don't feel anything," meant that my external *qi* simply went straight through him, because he was completely united with space. Master Zhao Guang was a true master. When we told him that he was like Lao-Zi, he smiled again, defecting our praise. Then, he raised his hand, crooked the little finger, and said, "Maybe just a little."

Limitless Qi

Master Zhao Guang said that he was in good health and that he had no interest in smoking or drinking. He pointed to me and said that I would understand what he meant. As the rest of the audience moved backward, Master Zhao Guang and I stood facing one another. I recalled very vividly the many hardships I had undergone in my efforts to establish the *qigong* method. These, however, were past, and I now knew supreme bliss. It was the greatest moment. Master Zhao Guang was aware of me from the beginning and he knew that I had been checking on him with *qi*.

According to Master Zhao Guang, the origin of *qi* is nothingness, and this is the origin which cannot be proved. The concept of emptiness in Buddhism and oblivion in Confucianism are the same, he said. His speech moved me deeply. Although we were listening to it in translation, I felt as if I could understand what he was saying directly, without an interpreter. After the speech a colleague and I asked him to write down a few words to commemorate the occasion. He chose phrases from Lao-Tzu. For me, he wrote, "Persistent non-desire will see the highest truth." For my collegue, it was "The gate to all truth is open to everyone."

When we left Xi-Yuan Hospital, we saw the clear sky spreading blue above us. I knew that my next journey had begun. My destination was transcendental-level *qigong*.

The Great Masters in China

In 1990, I was in Peking again to attend a seminar on mysticism and science when I met Master Yang Wen-Yen and Master Li Zhao-Sheng, both of China, who stated that their external *qi* was not diminished when they released *qi*. I was representing Japan and spoke about the Macrocosmic Orbit and the systematic techniques of *qi* based on the teachings of esoteric Shingon Buddhism.

While I was explaining the religious tools used in esoteric Buddhism—the single, three-pronged, and five-pronged vajras mentioned earlier—I released external *qi* with a five-pronged vajra as my silent message to the *qigong* practitioners who were able to use external *qi*. After my presentation, Master Yang Wen-Yen came over to speak to me and he had many kind things to say about my study of *qi* in esoteric Buddhism. He had been practicing Buddhist asceticism for many years. He put my rosary around his neck and meditated deeply for about ten minutes. When he handed it back to me, it was filled with excellent *qi* energy. He said that the rosary, together with my *qi*, would help me to heal patients. He has been treating patients free of charge for several decades as a form of almsgiving. I have heard that his patients are healed just by holding his prescriptions for Chinese herbs in their hands. I watched him write prescriptions after consulting with patients. He would place his hand on the piece of paper to release *qi* into his writing. To my surprise, I could actually smell the Chinese herbs when he laid his hand on the paper. He insisted that practitioners of *qigong* must have virtue. I had a sense that he was surrounded by many "thankful minds." I assume that this feeling must have derived from the many patients he has healed. This led me to think that when patients receive happiness, they feel thankful. When they are thankful, their mind energy actually returns to the person who has given them this happiness.

Master Li Zhao-Sheng, a teacher of a traditional Chinese fighting art, said that he liked the *qi* that I had released with a five-pronged vajra. He said to me, "When I felt your *qi*, a soldier appeared and my soul resonated." As a matter of fact, I released *qi* with the images of the God of Fire and the Buddha. They may have looked like soldiers to him. When he heard that I had been practicing Karate for many years, he said that he would think of me like a brother if I would oppose him in a bout. I was thankful for his great offer, but I refused. Who in his right mind would oppose him? He has been a martial arts expert since he was a child. He is as strong as an ox! Instead of sparring with him, I asked him about "visualization of the other self," which was the theme of his talk at the seminar. He told me that he could not tell me everything, because these principles were the esoteric teachings of his clan, but he showed me several mudras to use in my practice. These symbolic hand gestures are the core of secret practice. Mudras can promote the directional flow of *qi*. In return, I showed him my original mudra of spirals. I make it a principle to share with others any essential truths that I may find, so I have continued to show this mudra to my friends and patients for use in their meditation. "Visualization of the other self" is done in order to create another self, of *qi*, in the body, and then extend it outside the body so that it can be "seen." This is done by taking *qi* from earth and space; *qi* of this level is far beyond the level at which *qi* diminishes when it is released.

XII — How to Open Chakras and Absorb Qi from Space

Technical Revolution for Opening the Chakras

In order to open patients' Chakras, you must be able to collect large amounts of *qi* energy from the cosmic level, purify the negative *qi* that is blocking the flow of *qi* through the Chakras, and let pure *qi* flow into the Chakras. This unique method could be a technical revolution to open others' Chakras quickly. But this method can be performed only by advanced practitioners—that is, those who have mastered the Macrocosmic Orbit method.

You can open Chakras by yourself, too. After you master the Microcosmic Orbit method, practice the Macrocosmic Orbit method for several months. First you need to be able to sense the *qi* of the cosmic level yourself, then a strong imagination makes it possible to open your Chakras. Picture a glorious scene, in which *qi* of the cosmic level is flowing into you. Figure 12–1 gives you some idea of the process involved.

Figure 12–1
The Macrocosmic
Orbit method.

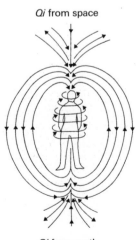

Qi from space

Qi from earth

The Macrocosmic Ring

When you have mastered the Macrocosmic Orbit method, and all your Chakras are open, you will be able to sense the quality of *qi*. At that point you will no longer be exhausted when you release *qi*. Many people have experienced this change, and it is a replicable result of mastering the Macrocosmic Orbit method. Replicability and verification are important elements in proving any scientific theory, including the Macrocosmic Orbit method. It is necessary, however, to know objectively whether or not one has mastered this method.

According to a vision that appeared while I was meditating, *qi* flows into the Chakras, spiralling clockwise. Thus I invented a ring that also makes the magnetic field spiral clockwise, incorporating the suggestions of a friend who was also studying *qigong*. I call it the "Macrocosmic Ring." Its use is quite simple.

Place the Macrocosmic Ring on top of your head (Bai-Hui) or under your coccyx (Xian-Gu) and you will feel *qi* flowing in; the Reflection of *Qi* Muscle Power test will also show that the strength of your fingers has increase. When the Macrocosmic Ring is placed in a way to make the magnetic field spin in a counterclockwise direction you will feel uncomfortable if any of your Chakras are not open, because the *qi* flow is obstructed. This blockage often leads to problems with physical and mental health. If all of your Chakras are open, the Reflection of *Qi* Muscle Power test will show that the strength of your fingers is not reduced, despite the stimulus of the counterclockwise magnetic field. Having tested several hundred people with both the Macrocosmic Ring and the Reflection of *Qi* Muscle Power test, I can conclude: those whose Bai-Hui and Xian-Gu Chakras are open will not be affected by the counterclockwise stimulus of the Macrocosmic Ring.

There are people whose Bai-Hui Chakra is open even before they receive any *qigong* training. They tend to be very intuitive or sensitive. Many women of this type are psychic and able to "see" invisible things. They tend to easily lose their balance physically, and are strongly influenced psychologically by other people's emotions. Those whose Xian-Gu Chakra is open are often great practitioners of the martial arts or very active entrepreneurs. It is not clear whether the open Chakra without training is *a priori* or *a posteriori*. Generally speaking, those who use their brain not only intellectually but also with full susceptibility have open Bai-Hui Chakra and those who are active and have strong limbs have open Xian-Gu Chakra.

What is the process whereby use of the Macrocosmic Ring lets us know whether the Chakras are open? I imagine that this process works because *qi* has a magnetic character and therefore, electromagnetic laws apply. My intuition that *qi* spins clockwise coincides with the law of right-handedness in electromagnetics (Figure 12–2). The Macrocosmic Ring serves as a stimulus to the Chakras only at the magnetic levels. I would recommend using the rings as a supportive device only after you are able to control external *qi* with the Macrocosmic Orbit method; otherwise, you may experience side effects.

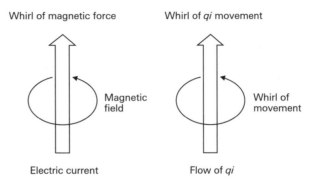

Figure 12–2
Magnetic spin and the spin of *qi*.

Space Is Full of Consciousness

Shuji Inomata, M.D., chief researcher of the Electric Technical Research Institute and president of the Japan Consciousness Engineering Organization, reports on *qi* from the viewpoint of New Age Science. He maintains that *qi* spirals clockwise. His basic proposition is: Consciousness/mind and mass/matter do not reciprocate directly. But when consciousness controls the current of physical time, positive and negative Shadow Energy flow in. There are two kinds of Shadow Energy: yin and yang. These are called *qi*, or prana, in Oriental philosophy. We have recently begun to consider possible practical uses of such energy. This suggests that the Oriental world view of the unity of consciousness and body is being put to practical use, despite the viewpoint taken by much of Western medicine that maintains that mind and body function independently. As the Heart Sutra notes, "Form is no other than emptiness, emptiness is no other than form" (for more on the Heart Sutra, see also page 145).

Therefore, the space around us, sometimes referred to as a "vacuum," is not empty space, despite widespread belief to the contrary. It is full of positive and negative Shadow Energy, or "consciousness," from which we can obtain unlimited energy. In Figure 12–3, Inomata shows the equation of consciousness, mass, and energy. Consciousness, shown here as Q, has been the focus of the traditions of religion and psychology alike. He explains that Q is pan-psychic consciousness— i.e., even a little rock on a country road has it. This is still more fundamental than the subconscious of Sigmund Freud or the collective unconscious of Carl Jung. However, my opinion is that it includes Jung's concepts of the collective unconscious and synchronicity. *Qigong* is a technique for controlling the mind and for allowing phenomena of energy to occur by using sensations of *qi*. For this purpose, needless to say, the Microcosmic Orbit method—which is an exercise intended to improve the physical health—is not enough. It is also absolutely necessary to master the Macrocosmic Orbit method.

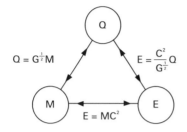

C: Speed of light
G: Gravitational constant
Q: Shadow electric charge (consciousness)
M: Gravity mass and inertial mass
E: Energy

Figure 12–3 Relationship among consciousness, mass, and energy.

Inomata states, "Scholars of Far Eastern studies insist that space is full of *qi*, or prana. Their theory can be called literature or philosophy, but that does not make it science." He explains complex electromagnetic theory in his book *Nyū saiensu no paradaimu* (New Age science paradigm). If I rephrase his views in my own words I would say that "*Qigong* practitioners insist that space is full of *qi*, or prana. Their theory can be called literature or philosophy, but that does not make it a real *qigong* method."

We are on the verge of a new era. I look forward to the day when people whose consciousness is remarkably advanced will be able to sense *qi* and heal one another, and when *qi* is generally accepted as a part of reality and as an instrument of greater awareness.

XIII — External Qi

Normalizing the Flow of Qi with Qigong

In this chapter I would like to consider the cause of disease and the role of *qigong* in medical treatment. Through my study of *Huang-Di Nei-Jing Su-Wen* ("The Yellow Emperor's classic of internal medicine"; referred to as *Su-Wen* from this point), I learned that classical Chinese medicine explains the cause of disease in this way: disease is generated when external conditions (a trigger) and internal conditions (a promoting state) coincide. According to *Su-Wen*, there are six external negative factors—wind, cold, dryness, humidity, heat, and fire—that act as triggers. Today, modern medicine would include in this list viruses and all manner of stress. Of course, these external conditions do not necessarily have the effect of making everyone ill. For instance, not everyone catches a cold when it is cold outside, and not everyone gets a stomachache from eating something rotten. But the homeostasis of an entire body is more likely to be compromised when adverse external conditions are present. This increased susceptibility, or vulnerability, provides an environment for disease to develop. In *Su-Wen*, this condition is expressed as the emptiness of Zheng-Qi, which refers to the operation of all the functions necessary for the body to maintain its normal condition. From the point of view of modern medicine, the functions involved in maintaining homeostasis would include the immune system, the hormonal system, and the autonomic nervous system; it is energy which maintains all these systems. You may wonder though, how the emptiness of Zheng-Qi occurs. According to *Su-Wen*, the basic causes are improper diet, exhaustion, curvature of the spine, and psychological stress. These factors are the most important to take into account. In addition, *Su-Wen* stresses the importance of the physical surroundings and climate.

It may be difficult to do anything immediately to change one's physical surroundings. Moving to a new climate is not usually a practical option. But there are things that you can consider. The three basic factors in the rise of disease—diet, exhaustion, and the seven emotions—can be changed without great difficulty. (The "seven emotions" is a concept from both Buddhism and Chinese medicine; these emotions are pleasure, anger, sorrow, fear, love, hatred, and desire.) Chinese medicine includes a vast dietary system for treatment and prevention of disease. For exhaustion or curvature of the spine, the moving *qigong* method (physical *qigong* exercise such as the Microcosmic Orbit method) should be helpful. The inactive *qigong* method (meditation), will be useful for psychological or emotional stress. Understanding the etiology of disease is essential to finding out what is wrong with a patient. You should be able automatically to ascertain the pathological cause—whether it be a curved spine, improper diet, or psychological stress.

On the other hand, you may think that a patient has been affected by a combination of causes. In that case you could suggest that he or she try taking a drug from either the Western or the Chinese medical traditions. You could supply dietary guidelines, or recommend that the patient join a *qigong* class. Recent research shows that Chinese herbs can be effective in improving the functioning of various systems within the body, including the immune system, the hormonal system, and the autonomic nervous system. While Western drugs or surgical treatment are very effective against external causes or current symptoms, Chinese medicine also plays a role in restoring balance within the organism. *Qigong* or a dietary cure can help to normalize the human body and prevent illness. Recognition of the benefits to be gained from different traditions is one example of what I call "mandala thinking," which holds that different elements can be positioned in terms of their relative importance within the whole.

Mind Is Power

I believe that the *qigong* method is not just physical exercise but a very beneficial training system for the attainment of greater human spirituality.

If you are practicing external *qi* in order to heal patients, you must understand all the following points.

1. The purpose of training to use external *qi* is to realize that mind forms energy. Through your experiences you will realize that *qi* energy acts on matter, organic things, and circumstances.

2. To learn the technique for obtaining information on external *qi* is also a good form of training to increase the power of the mind.

3. Training in advanced *qigong* for external *qi* is quite free and unrestricted. Neither a license nor the authorization of any school is necessary.

4. If you release external *qi* with the Microcosmic Orbit method, you are likely to be tired afterwards. This problem can be resolved, however, by mastering the Macrocosmic Orbit method, which does not produce fatigue.

Patients who want to receive external *qi* must understand the following:

1. You should train yourself. Receiving external *qi* from others is only a supporting activity which helps to fill the emptiness of Zheng-Qi.

2. You can also activate your inner *qi* with *qigong* exercise. (Developing your *qi* will help you to use external *qi*.)

Opinion is divided on external *qi*. Some say that it is a paranormal ability that has curative powers. On the other hand, some *qigong* practitioners insist that external *qi* should not be the main goal; instead we should aim to cultivate inner *qi*.

I would like to emphasize that anyone can train to use external *qi*. External *qi* is a universal power hidden in everyone. The first requirement is desire. Training will then awaken this hidden ability. Receiving information from external *qi* will be beneficial for your mind power. Releasing external *qi* will be a very effective training method for recognizing the existence of mind energy. When external *qi* becomes like second-nature to you, you will notice how meaningless it is to even discuss whether using external *qi* requires some special ability.

Muneyuki Nishiyama, M.D., a *qi* practitioner in Saitama, Japan, has written about his experiences in healing with external *qi*. He uses external *qi* without becoming exhausted; on the contrary, he says, he often feels elated. He writes that, "Desperate patients suffering from what are usually considered incurable diseases often travel great distances to visit me. When I am ready to treat a patient, the Goddess of Mercy appears in front of the patient. Sometimes the healing Buddha enters my body; then I become just a vessel for the Buddha, and my self disappears. I feel so thankful, and my eyes fill with tears. This happens often. As a matter of fact, I sometimes am confused by these extraordinary sensations, because they make the world so rich and vibrant."

Nishiyama's *qi* level is beyond categorization in terms of the of the Macrocosmic or Macrocosmic Orbit methods. When he releases external *qi* for his patients, he may of course be observing the unseen world, and yet a part of him—another self—is also calmly observing the entire scene. It is as if two computers—one of *qi* and one of reality—were functioning simultaneously in his mind. Actually it is very important to control these two computers, when involved in the *qi* world. I began to learn *qi* because I wanted to use external *qi* to help patients, so I know what Nishiyama means when he speaks of his eyes filling with tears. A sense of deep susceptibility is the essence of *qigong*. Training in the use of external *qi* reminds us that as human beings we interact at all levels of existence of the external world.

XIV — Standing Zen

What Is Standing Zen?

In 1975, when I was a student and practicing Karate every day, *qigong* was still completely unknown in Japan. I was eager to improve in my martial arts ability and I spent a good deal of time each day reading books and trying all kinds of new techniques. I realized that mental training was necessary as well, so I was also studying Yoga and the mysteries of esoteric Buddhism. Then I read a book by Ken'ichi Sawai about a Chinese martial art that supposedly allowed people to maintain their physical strength even into old age. Called Taikiken, it was brought to Japan by Sawai after he had studied the martial arts in China. Sawai's philosophy on training was completely new to me. Until that time I had collected information mainly from quite practical books on Karate or kinesiology. Conventional training in Karate involved repeating the same movement as many times as possible, so that the body learns to perform it easily; the muscles are then strengthened by gradually increasing the load placed on them.

There are two basic kinds of training in Taikiken: one is Standing Zen, which involves standing absolutely still; the other, Hai, is a back-and-forth, rocking movement with the hands held at the same level as the face. By practicing Standing Zen for hours each day, it is possible to develop *qi* power, and to maintain this power into old age. Sawai's teacher, Wang Xiang-Qi, was an elderly man, while Sawai was young and full of energy and was a master of Judo and Kendo (traditional Japanese fencing) as well. Yet Sawai was never able to get the better of his old master. I wondered how it was that practice in Hai and Standing Zen could produce such phenomenal power. I began practicing these exercises, to learn for myself how they work.

At first Standing Zen gave me nothing but aching muscles. Standing Zen is a *qigong* method designed as a form of training in the martial arts, and very different from ordinary *qigong* (see Figure 14–1). The waist needed to be positioned low, and I was able to hold that stance for only a few minutes at first. I lacked patience, and often thought about giving up the training, but whenever I opened his book, my enthusiasm returned. After about six months, I was able to hold the position for half an hour. And then one day, while I was practicing Karate, I suddenly noticed that my movement had improved. Until that time, I had concentrated only on the speed of my footwork. But now I was holding my waist in that same slightly lowered position, which made my movements in general and my responses to the opponent more fluid and efficient. I was able to do "circular," rather than simple straight-line, movements. I was very happy to find that my experience with Standing Zen was having a noticeable effect on my ability in the martial arts.

Stand with your legs spread just a bit, so that they are the same width as your shoulders, and with your toes pointing slightly inward. Release any tension from your heels, knees, and the tops of your thighs. Keeping your back straight, breathe in and pull your chest up. Your arms should be at your sides and your fingertips aligned, as you then relax, so that your arms are not lying flat against your trunk, but are hanging free. When you feel *qi* enter and settle into the balls of your feet, concentrate on absorbing that *qi*—like water from the earth—straight up into your arms. When the *qi* reaches your shoulders, you should feel the weight leave your arms. At that point, raise your arms out horizontally and continue to breathe naturally for a while.

Figure 14–1

Standing Zen as Qigong

Why does Standing Zen—a standing position in which the waist is held low—have such a great effect, despite being initially painful?

Standing Zen is not easy at first. Your thighs and your knees will hurt. Your arms may begin to feel like iron weights; after a while, your abdomen or your back may start hurting at well. Many parts of your body will ache, and you will be inclined to stop sooner rather than later. But remember, even though it may seem like a constant struggle, in fact your subconsciousness gradually makes your muscles adapt. From the point of view of kinesiology, your muscles contract when you maintain one posture for a long period. The increased fatigue caused by the strain on your muscles will definitely make you feel a certain amount of pain. If you have strong muscles, you will be able to avoid fatigue. This reliance on physical strength is the basis of Western weight training. But in Standing Zen, you train the motor center of the brain to hold your muscles in a contracted state. It means that you are also training the signal processing system that encompasses the nerve cells of the brain, the spinal cord, and the muscles (Figure 14–2).

MA = Motor area   H = Hypothalamus   SB = Small brain

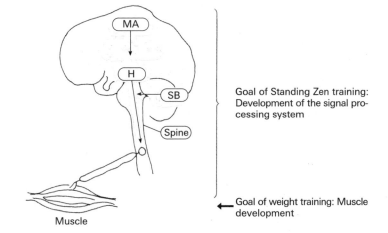

Figure 14–2
Standing Zen training versus weight training.

Goal of Standing Zen training: Development of the signal processing system

Goal of weight training: Muscle development

Muscle

To be brief, while weight training strengthens the "motor," Standing Zen strengthens the "electric current" and the "electric line" in order to obtain increased power from the "motor." In the laboratory, stimulation of the synapse circuits and nerve muscular junctions is known to make nerve information flow more smoothly. This is called the phenomenon of facilitation.

Endorphins and Qigong

You will notice that you begin to feel a pleasant sensation at a certain point in your practice of Standing Zen. I have experienced an amazing feeling of uplift on the last day of a tough Karate training camp after I practiced Standing Zen, despite being completely exhausted before. I was amazed at how much power I found that I still had. But the sensations that I derived from Standing Zen were qualitatively different than the simple uplift that I experienced in the Karate training camp.

In Standing Zen, at first you notice that your mind is very clear. Since your whole body is relaxed, you feel as if there is an axis running straight through your body. The feeling is something like a top that is standing straight while turning at high speed, or like becoming pure consciousness and no longer feeling your physical body. There then comes a moment when you suddenly get a new idea, or come up with an answer you have been seeking.

It seems that endorphin is the substance that changes a suffering or painful sensation into a pleasant one. Endorphins are neurotransmitters produced by the brain that behave as pain regulators and are also thought to contribute to euphoric feelings. Acupuncture is a stimulus that can promote the release of endorphins. You may have heard before about the method of administering anesthesia with acupuncture that was invented recently by *qigong* master Lin Hou-Shen in China. At one point, this was considered a wonder, but since the discovery of endorphins it is easily explained.

People practice asceticism in various disciplines, including Yoga, the martial arts, and many religions. Endorphins produced in the brain as a result of ascetic practices help to alter practitioners' consciousness. But the clear consciousness achieved in Standing Zen is not caused solely by endorphins, but also by dopamine, which is the single most important neurotransmitter for awakening pleasant sensations and creative impulses in the brain. Before I explain in the next chapter how dopamine functions, I would like to introduce the correct way to practice Standing Zen (see also Figure 14–1).

How to practice Standing Zen

1. Relax your feet, knees, and the inguinal region. Relax the chest and throat. The most important thing here is to open the acupuncture point Ming-Men (on the back, at the same height as the navel).

2. Your arms will rise of their own accord when *qi* starts to flow through them. You will then start to feel that your arms are weightless.

3. Find your center of gravity, and the proper position for your hips, by swinging your arms back and forth slightly, and then stand still. (Your waist should be held rather low.)

4. Exhale with your mouth open. After a short pause keep exhaling the rest of the air in three short breaths, with your lips rounded, as if you were blowing out a candle. Then inhale naturally. When you repeat this breathing method, your breathing will slow considerably.

5. Concentrate on making a *qi* ball or on circulating *qi* through your body with the Microcosmic or Macrocosmic Orbit methods. (This is essential for using *qi* energy freely.)

Notes

1. Before you begin doing Standing Zen, perform *qigong* exercises (the Microcosmic Orbit method) since this relaxes the body and helps to adjust the backbone.

2. Don't forget to do some kind of exercise like stretching or taking a short walk at the end of your practice. You must quickly bring your consciousness back from the *qi* stage to the real world. While you are in a state of deep meditation produced by the practice of Standing Zen, the mind seems to influence deep parts of the brain.

If you stand too rigidly, you will not be able to practice abdominal breathing easily because your Ming-Men will be closed (Figure 14–3). When Ming-Men is open, you can breathe easily and *qi* energy is free to flow through the whole body. If you do not open Ming-Men, Standing Zen becomes pure torture. Not only that, but bad posture can also damage your back or your inner organs. For instance, wearing high-heeled shoes forces you to stand "at attention" and has the effect of keeping Ming-Men closed. Wearing this type of shoe can lead to back pain or autonomic imbalance caused by shallow breathing.

Another reason that I recommend Standing Zen is that this discipline makes it easy to avoid earthy thoughts. This point distinguishes it from most forms of meditation.

Figure 14–3
Breathing when Ming-Men is open or closed.

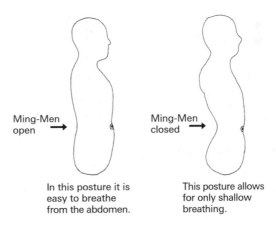

Ming-Men open →

Ming-Men closed →

In this posture it is easy to breathe from the abdomen.

This posture allows for only shallow breathing.

XV — Qi as the Missing Link Between Nerve and Brain Function

What Is the A-10 Nerve?

Japanese pharmacologist Kosuke Oki has written extensively about the relationship between brain activity and stimulation received though the soles of the feet: "The activity of the A-10 nerve is worth noting, particularly in connection to healthy brain functioning and learning ability. The reason for this is that human creativity occurs at times of the A-10 nerve's overactivity. Creativity evolves by means of the A-10 nerve, through an excess of awareness and pleasurable sensations. Creativity and pleasurable sensations act in concert and are inseparable. I think that activating the A-10 nerve is an extremely effective form of brain training. In order to activate this nerve, you need to train yourself physically, so that your body becomes ready, whenever necessary, to secrete important hormones such as proopiomelanocortin (POMC), which is a crucial resource of vital energy and stamina ... Walking and running are both good forms of training for the health of the brain. The strongest stimulation of the sensory nerves throughout the body is that received through the muscles of the feet. Stimulation received through the feet invigorates the sensory A and B nerves, which in turn stimulates the brain.

The effects of *qigong* training are deeply linked to brain functioning, and so in order to clarify why *qigong* is so important, I would like to take a moment to explain the functioning of the brain in a bit more detail.

The effect of *qigong* originates in the brain. The A-10 nerve originates at the midbrain of the brain stem (Figure 15–1). It runs to the hypothalamus, which generates primitive feelings of "desire," and stretches to the limbic system, or the animal brain, whose origins are ancient even in comparison to other parts of the cerebrum, and which controls the production of emotions. From there, the A-10 nerve enters a part of the neocortex—which is the seat of intelligence and higher learning. The A-10 nerve also branches out to the hippocampus that is involved in memory and learning, and further connects to the nucleus accumbens of the limbic system which is said to play a role in the vital functions and in the instinct for self-preservation. Finally, it extends to the frontal association area of the neocortex that controls powers of creativity.

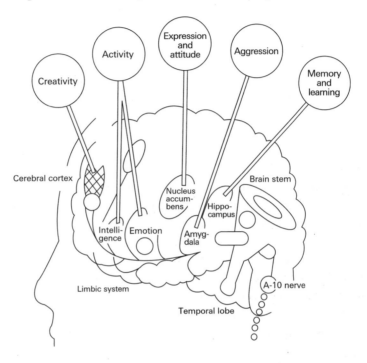

Figure 15–1
Simple diagram of the anatomy of the brain.

The A-10 Nerve and Ecstasy

The A-10 nerve is sometimes called the "hedonic nerve" because of its connection with pleasure. Since this nerve extends from the hypothalamus to the frontal association area of the neocortex, it controls sensations of pleasure of every kind, ranging from pleasure in eating or sexual activity to creativity and even complete enlightenment. Dopamine is the neurotransmitter for the A-10 nerve. Futhermore, the A-10 nerve lacks any autoreceptor, which would normally act as a "braking system," controlling negative feedback in and around the frontal association area of the neocortex. Oki writes, "Dopamine acts in the association area of the frontal lobe differently than it does in other parts of the brain. Experimental results surprised me. Here is my hypothesis on creativity: Sufficient secretion of dopamine frees a human being to practice trial and error, and allows the creativity full play. If my hypothesis holds true, the theory that excess secretion of dopamine causes mental disease and schizothymia could be correct, and the old saying, 'No great genius was ever without an element of madness' can be seen to have a neurophysical component."

Oki states that the A-10 nerve controls the sensations of pleasure—which are a basic, guiding principle for humans—encompassing sexual desire and the appetite for food as well as the desire for enlightenment.

The Brain Mechanisms Involved in Qi Energy

Proopiomelanocortin (POMC) is said to be the origin of physical stamina and of *qi* energy. When human beings and animals experience stress, the protein POMC is produced in the hypothalamus and the pituitary gland (Figure 15–2). It is then broken down by enzymes into three kinds of small-scale proteins: beta-endorphins, adrenocorticotrophic hormone (ACTH), and the adrenocortical growth-factor. ACTH stimulates the adrenal cortex, resulting in the secretion of adrenocortial hormone, which alleviates physical stress caused by inflammation, allergies, and the like. Beta-endorphins act against mental stress through their painkilling properties, while also evoking pleasant sensations. Adrenocortial growth-factor supports ACTH in its work of stimulating the adrenal glands. It ensures that we have a mechanism in the brain to overcome stress and to gain additional endurance and *qi* energy as needed.

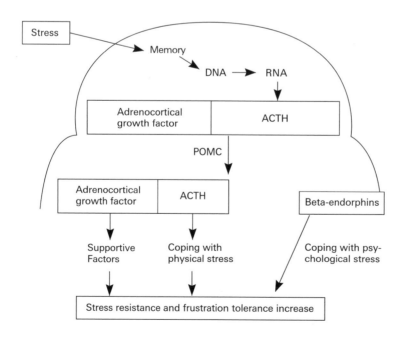

Figure 15–2
Mechanisms of hormone regulation.

When you practice Standing Zen, you will experience some pain in your trunk, legs, and arms. But if you bear the pain and maintain the position, you will come to feel a different, pleasant sensation. You may also have flashes of intuition about problems that have been on your mind. Standing Zen is said to activate the A-10 nerve and POMC, stimulating our *qi* energy and creativity. This is a way to theoretically prove the effectiveness of Standing Zen.

Genuine Pleasure from Qigong

When your ability to experience pleasant sensations weakens, illness will occur. This is why you need to train your "hedonic nerve," or the A-10 nerve, with *qigong*.

In modern society, we experience all kinds of stress, both physical and mental. But if we produce sufficient ACTH and beta-endorphins, we can overcome stress, turning it into what I call "pleasant stress." If we do not, the adrenal cortex may malfunction and mental or physical depression occur, leading eventually to illness. In order to avoid becoming ill, it is important to know how to achieve pleasurable sensations.

If you experience sensations of pleasure from daily *qigong* exercise, you will gradually stop doing things that make you uncomfortable.

From the viewpoint of energy expenditure, I recommend Standing Zen, unless you are full of energy and eager to practice asceticism. If you do want to practice asceticism, remember that this practice is not itself the goal, but is only a means of approaching the goal. Some ascetics with great self-confidence and hard training, begin competing with one another. When they do this, however, they begin to rely on their own power. This is different from advanced *qigong* training, in which the Macrocosmic Orbit method eventually allows you to receive *qi* energy from space and release it to patients. In my own *qigong* classes, I have found that some ascetics have a hard time sensing *qi* with the Macrocosmic Orbit method, while some beginners who know nothing about *qigong* are able to master the Macrocosmic Orbit method quickly. There are some people who practice rigorous asceticism. When they are close to death, they may finally become aware of external *qi*, but this is a long and unnecessarily arduous route.

Learn what pleasurable sensations are. Our brain has a system leading us toward progress, based on genuine pleasure.

Don't forget, either, the connection between the brain and the immune system, when studying *qigong*. We need to do more detailed research on why it is possible to heal illness through *qigong*. This issue is being hotly debated in the medical world today. It is clear that the "hypothalamic pituitary gland adrenal cortex system" interacts with the immune system through adrenocortial hormones, and that neurotransmitter receptors for adrenaline, noradrenaline and acetylcholine influence lymphocytes directly, through the autonomic nervous system. In the future, studies of the underlying brain mechanisms may allow us to successfully heal patients, without relying on "medicine" as we know it now. But even before that point, we can practice the *qigong* which the ancients bequeathed us as a tradition for maintaining our physical and emotional well-being. I am sure that the secrets of the brain will be illuminated someday.

Oki writes, "The brain is like an enormous chemical computer which runs on chemical substances called neurotransmitters. The human mind will be made clear in the near future, with a scientific explanation of its physical workings."

My opinion is a little different from Oki's on this point. He focuses much more on the importance of the "physical workings" of the brain. I would suggest that any effort to "explain" the brain with reference to only the physical dimension is doomed to failure. That is why I believe that continued research into the unseen world of *qi* is extremely important.

XVI — Imagination and Visualization

Developing the Imagination

You do not need to believe in the existence of gods or the Buddha to practice the *qigong* method. *Qigong* as I describe and advocate it is based on physical and spiritual techniques from the martial arts, the medical arts, esoteric Buddhism, Taoism, and Confucianism—but with any doctrinal elements removed. However, if you have studied Buddhism, you may understand the progress you make toward achieving the essence of *qi* in "Buddhist" terms or imagery. This may happen with Buddhism, or with any of the traditions that are sources of *qigong*.

You may feel uneasy about becoming involved with anything that seems to have some connection to the gods, the Buddha, or similar figures. But if you concentrate singlemindedly on the idea of an existence beyond yourself, you will come face-to-face with the limits of your own external *qi*, and may very well "see" this higher existence appear before you, or feel it enter you. Experiences of this sort should be viewed merely as a sign of the tremendous powers of visualization and imagination.

We need to consider here the relationship between imagination and quality of *qi*. When you are able to make a *qi* ball between your palms, practice changing its quality with your imagination. The following are two exercises that will help you develop your powers of imagination.

The rising sun

Early in the morning, practice *qigong* while looking at the sun soon after it rises. If possible, practice either the Microcosmic or Macrocosmic Orbit method. You will also benefit simply from standing and watching the sun rise. The morning sun is not so dazzling. When you inhale the air, imagine that you are absorbing golden light from the morning sun through Bai-Hui on the crown of your head and Yin-Tang on your forehead. Your whole body is now shining in gold, from the ends of your hair down into your head, neck, arms, chest, back, upper and lower abdomen, your legs, and even as far as the tips of your toes.

Close your eyes, and feel the morning sun shining vividly on your mental "screen." Now the golden sun enters your *qi* ball. When your imagination grows strong enough, you will be able to practice this no matter where you are or what time of day it is.

Rich green earth

Practice the *qigong* method while standing in a green, grassy spot. Inhale the *qi* of the earth through the soles of your feet and through Xien-Gu on your back in much the same way you did in the previous exercise. Imagine the *qi* ball also turning green. If you can do this, the *qi* sensation between your palms will be ready to change into whatever you imagine: the morning sun, the green earth, the bright full moon, or exploding magma. You can imagine anything. If you want to increase the effectiveness of this training, try it with some *qi* friends. Place your hand between your friend's palms and feel the *qi* ball. You will notice that the sensation of the *qi* ball changes as your images of it change. Take turns altering the color, and having the other person guess what color the ball is. You will be surprised by the high rate of correct answers.

Changing the Quality of Qi

In healing, the *qi* of the bright full moon is equivalent to "Xi" (Chinese; saline land) in Chinese medicine, which can be used for calming overexcitement or lowering a high fever. On the other hand, the golden morning sunlight is "Bu" (Chinese; repair), and is generally used for treating various malfunctions. The *qi* of the morning sun is extremely effective in improving health, and not only as a training for external *qi*.

By the way, you may wonder whether external *qi* can be used destructively. In fact, this is possible. For example, if you release external *qi* in anger, the receiver will suffer. But this will also return to you in the form of poorer physical and mental health. There is nothing wrong with becoming angry. We all lose our tempers now and then; this is only natural. I do want to caution you, though, not to release external *qi* in a state of anger, since this is destructive to all.

After you master the technique of releasing external *qi* with color images, practice releasing *qi* while visualizing any image that you consider sublime, such as the gods, the Buddha, or any great personage from ages past. Feel the way that the *qi* sensations and your emotions change in accordance with the objects that you call to mind. It will be also interesting to practice sensing these things as colors. With practice, you will probably learn to see auras.

How to Make Your Wishes Come True

I mentioned previously that physical *qigong* exercise was necessary to increase the volume of *qi*. This is true, but only to a certain level, until you master the Microcosmic Orbit method and the early stage of the Macrocosmic Orbit method. At later stages, the main emphasis is on mental training. I learned this by teaching medical doctors and business executives in *qigong* seminars. I opened their Chakras when I thought they were ready to practice on a higher level, so that they could learn what the Macrocosmic Orbit method was like. It didn't take them long to learn to use external *qi*, but I realized that they still needed to practice the Microcosmic Orbit method in order to increase the volume of their *qi*. Mastery of the Macrocosmic Orbit method can be compared to the evolution of the mind, whereas the Microcosmic Orbit method is like a base camp for climbing high mountains. When you run into trouble on your way to the summit—the summit in this case being the Macrocosmic Orbit method—you can always return to base camp, or the Microcosmic Orbit method.

Your wishes will come true when you are able to clearly visualize them and when you are convinced they will come true. This great rule is so simple, clear, practical, and effective that it is almost almighty; what's more, it has no side effects. Specialists in the theme of "success in life" like Napoleon Hill, Joseph Murphy, and Paul Mayer have written dozens of books on this subject. The rule can be summed up in just two words: "imagination and conviction."

You can practice by yourself and increase your powers of imagination by making a *qi* ball and then changing its color or making it circulate through your body. You should be able to feel the actual *qi* sensation, which distinguishes this from other forms of training of the imagination. It is difficult, naturally, to maintain a particular image in the mind for any length of time. Normally all sorts of rambling thoughts will arise, pushing other images aside. But if you are able to sense *qi*, images will stay with you for a longer time, and with practice you will be able to make them increasingly clear.

I have heard that professional chess players are able to reproduce an entire game afterward from memory without the slightest effort. Recently I am able to recall the operations that I perform from beginning to end, almost as if I had recorded them on video. This makes it much easier for me to visualize my next operation step-by-step, and has made me a better surgeon. When I was still a beginner in *qigong*, my "video playback" function didn't work very well, because it was often interrupted by rambling thoughts.

As these examples suggest, clarity of mind and an imagination that has some staying power play a large role in intelligence. Making a *qi* ball, practicing the Microcosmic and Macrocosmic Orbit methods, and learning to use external *qi* are all excellent ways to expand the powers of imagination.

Conviction is also important. Yukio Funai, a management consultant with the think tank Funai Institute in Tokyo, states, "In order to actualize your wish, you must imagine the results of it and be convinced that it will be fully realized. When you are sick and want to return to health, you must keep in mind a clear image of yourself as already healthy. Draw a picture of yourself as a healthy person in your mind and look at it every day. But visualization alone is not enough; you must also be convinced that you will return to good health. Many intellectuals who are accustomed to relying primarily on reason tend to doubt this method, and if you are one of them, unfortunately your wish will not come true."

If you have difficulty imagining the result that you want, try autosuggestion or self-hypnotism before you go to bed or right after you wake up. This may help you to overcome your own resistance. You must allow the image to infiltrate the deep layers of your mind.

Using *qigong* is another way to help make your wishes come true. *Qigong* can demonstrate to you clearly and quickly that mind energy—that is, external *qi*—acts on matter and living things, and has the power to change reality. When you begin to experience the same results every time you practice, you will gain confidence in using external *qi*. Even simple forms of training, like changing the taste of drinks, will be useful. When you are able to feel *qi*, first try this experiment alone. When you are sure of your own ability, perform first for just your friends, and then later for people who are doubtful about external *qi*.

Many people give up their wishes too easily. Remain convinced that things will happen slowly but surely, and do not become negative about yourself. If you keep on practicing this method, what you wish for will eventually come true, just the way a seed planted in soil begins to grow, completely unseen, and when the time comes finally blooms.

Cultivating External Qi

Learning to use external *qi* is also very effective in helping us realize the things we wish for. People who come to my lectures often ask whether external *qi* is something that anyone can learn to use. I always answer that it is, but only if the person's will is strong enough to continue practicing the exercise faithfully. The two other requirements are imagination and firm belief.

In order to develop your imagination and your conviction, you will need to do all the following.

1. Start small and practice. For instance, beginners should start with something as simple as changing the taste of food or drinks.

2. Take on more difficult matters little by little.

3. Look for sensible people who understand you, so that you can enjoy a constructive rivalry with them.

4. Bear in mind that you are simply trying to awaken a hidden ability that everyone has.

   There is nothing mysterious or extraordinary about the skill of releasing external *qi*. It is only about as difficult as learning to play a musical instrument, to swim, or to cook. It is possible to learn to release external *qi* even without understanding the theory behind it—for example, by aligning yourself with a teacher or chanting to the god of your religion. However, if you do not understand the theory, it will be difficult to set new goals for yourself and to reach new levels. It will be difficult to overcome problems you may encounter. What is more, a lack of theoretical understanding can cause you to depend too heavily on a teacher who acts like a religious leader.

   The goal of *qi* exercise is to unite with the *qi* of the universe, without depending on anyone or anything. You may want to rely on your teacher at the beginning, but you must conquer your dependence as soon as possible. Avoid any "teacher" who tries to frighten you by mentioning a curse or such things. If you are teaching external *qi*, you must have as a top priority the goal of leading students to independence.

   I suggest that you do not speak unnecessarily about the mysteries of the *qi* world, and that you tend to keep the information secret.

5. Maintain an attitude of inquisitiveness and scientific inquiry. Be sure to reconsider and check any results that you see. For instance, prepare two portions of a given food, and release *qi* into one of them, so that you can compare the difference in taste.

6. Watch and imitate more advanced practitioners. This process of imitating will allow you to improve your ability to accurately recognize and imagine. Thus it will help you to become better at visualization.

7. Begin to do away with your negative thoughts on the impossibility of success.

8. Use your five ordinary senses, as well as your *qi* sense, when you visualize.

Perception will occur with the five senses, so heightening of perception is especially important. When the *qi* sense is added to your five senses, your ability to perceive objects correctly is heightened, and your imaginative ability can develop. When the *qi* sense is added to the tactual sense that reacts only through touch, you can sense warmth, pressure, tingling, or electricity on your palms, which means that your ability to receive *qi* has improved. As a doctor of Chinese medicine, I often take my patients' pulse. From the pulse alone I can tell a great deal about a patient's current condition—including appetite and the state of the autonomic nervous system. I would suggest that this is an example of what happens when perception is heightened.

I have friends who practice *qi* and who work as musicians, cooks, or painters. They tell me that *qi* energy is present in sound, in taste, and in colors. According to them, the more *qi* they feel, the better the results. When artists concentrate intently on a certain thing, the five senses are sharpened, and the *qi* sense also develops at the same time.

Now, how is an image related to the five senses? When you hear the word "image," you may think of the ordinary visual sense and try to "see" in the usual way. But in fact that is not enough.

When you do visualization, try to add elements that employ other senses; add details about the sound, touch, taste, or even the aroma of the scene. When you practice Standing Zen, imagine that you are looking at the rising sun. The golden sun at the ridgeline of a mountain is blessing you, warming your entire body with its soft rays of light. Your body is now shining golden.

Listen to the wind and the birds. Take in the smell of the fresh air and the trees all around you. Enjoy the texture of the trunk of your favorite tree.

If you find it difficult to visualize in this much detail, climb a mountain yourself first. Then you will be able to "recall" the surroundings, and this will make it easier to visualize. When you can visualize well, you will be able to practice Standing Zen anywhere, at any time. Enter and wander through the world or a picture of painting. Clear images held in the mind's eye can create a new reality.

I know a few people who are gifted with very strong powers of imagination, making them truly psychic. One such person is Toshihide Hisamura, whose extraordinary abilities I will discuss in the next chapter. I have visited him more than twenty times, and each time have been completely amazed at his ability. For example, he can make objects float. It seems that he releases power with a very clear image in mind, while assuming that a certain phenomenon has already occurred. When he wishes to make objects float in the air, for instance, he creates a clear image in his mind, in which the object is first stationery, and then rises. As soon as the object actually seen overlaps with the one visualized, the physical object begins to float. Needless to say, his powers of imagination are far beyond the ordinary.

Why Do We Need to Control External Qi?

When I use external *qi* for my patients, I look at the backbone through the clothes and can "see" its curve as an image. Then I release external *qi* to the abnormally curved part, with the image in mind of a normal back. Advanced *qi* practitioners can correct curved backbones in this way and activate a patient's *qi* flow of the Microcosmic Orbit. Symptoms such as back pain begin to diminish. The effect is apparent to the patient, and can also be checked with thermography and with the AMI machine that measures meridian energy.

Consciousness, matter, and physical energy all have vibration. When you succeed in achieving consciousness—or a clear image in your brain—this generates a creative pattern of vibration that can cause phenomena such as floating or materialization. I would suggest that the vibration of this energy is a pattern or mold that forms the physical world.

When you make efforts to improve your ability to visualize, your creativity will also naturally be increased. Adding an element of *qigong* training will be the fastest route to greater ability to visualize. When you train your visualization ability with the *qi* sense which is invisible but can still be sensed, the *qi* sense blocks the appearance of other thoughts and holds the image stable, preventing it from suddenly being displaced from the mind. When you have succeeded in improving your visualization ability and your ability to control external *qi*, as well as in increasing your firm belief, you will understand intuitively why I have been explaining about external *qi* from many different angles (Figure 16–1).

The human being does not exist only as a physical body, but also as a body of *qi* energy. When you recognize that all people exchange *qi* with one another, your consciousness will naturally evolve. When you are able to absorb or to release external *qi* freely with opened Chakras, you will know that you are alive and that you are permitted to live in the universe. With this you will be awakened to universal consciousness.

Development of enhanced abilities	Evolution of consciousness
Five senses and the *qi* sense	Humans as physical beings
↓ Five senses (including conscious abilities) enhanced	↓ Humans with body of *qi* energy
↓ Enhanced visualization ability, with the five senses fully functioning	↓ Awareness of other forms of existence that have *qi* energy
↓ Evolution of extraordinary visualization ability	↓ Awareness of unlimited *qi* in space and of how to make it flow
	↓ Awareness of universal consciousness

Figure 16–1
Results that can be obtained from *qi* training.

XVII — Energy of Consciousness in Science and Medicine

Inomata's Theory

No one has yet succeeded in measuring *qi* energy on a strictly physical level. But *qi*'s effect on human beings can be confirmed with the Reflection of *Qi* Muscle Power test or the breathing method. These methods are now effective and replicable. *Qi* training includes the Reflection of *Qi* Muscle Power test, hand-dowsing, and radiesthesia using pendulums. Releasing *qi* energy refers to training in the Macrocosmic Orbit method. However, the basic theory that would explain the phenomena of *qi* from a scientific point of view has not yet been found. A great deal of useful information is available on techniques for *qi* training and health, but one should also consider a universal model that would explain the phenomena of *qi*.

The term "model" as I use it here refers to a theoretical construction that would provide a reasonable explanation on the basis of known facts. Therefore, a good model predicts the phenomena that are included in the structure. Its replicability can be a useful judgement of the effectiveness of the model. The model should not conflict with the laws of physics.

One theory which satisfies all these conditions is that proposed by Shuji Inomata, which I introduced earlier, in Chapter XII. As was mentioned, this theory allows us to logically systematize various psychic phenomena such as telekinesis, ESP, telepathy, and psychic phenomena, and other mysterious experiences. They can be considered manifestations of different evolutionary branches of higher-level consciousness.

Let me explain Inomata's theory briefly (Figure 17–1). $E = mc^2$ is the formula discovered by Einstein for the conversion of matter into physical energy. It is also the basic formula for constructing an atomic bomb. Prior to Einstein, it had been thought that matter and physical energy could not be converted into one another. But since his formula was verified with high accuracy by nuclear reactions and the atomic bomb, the idea that matter and physical energy can be converted into one another has been completely accepted in the world of physics. The universe consists of matter and physical energy. Inomata adds to this equation one more element—that of consciousness. In religion and psychology, consciousness had already been accepted as a main theme, but its relation to matter and physical energy had never been explained.

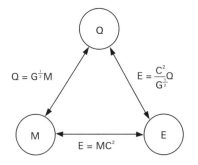

Q: Consciousness
M: Matter
E: Physical energy
G: Gravity
C: Speed of light

Figure 17–1
Inomata's theory.

In Buddhism, the things of this world are thought to be more reflections of consciousness. Inomata expresses this same idea theoretically, with a numerical formula. To me this is a hopeful sign, suggesting that consciousness may someday be accepted in science and medicine, which would bring untold benefits to all humankind.

Inomata emphasizes that it is time to study medicine that includes consciousness. The term "consciousness" as he uses it is not identical to the general usage of the word. For him it has a pantheistic meaning, and encompasses even stones or trees. This concept of consciousness is in fact quite similar to the basic concept of *qi*. When physics developed, the world changed. But Western medicine is still controlled, to this day, by Newtonian physics. We are not aware of the energy of consciousness that we as human beings have.

Incidentally, I asked him how he originally conceived this theory. He said that he had been watching one of Yuri Geller's spoon-bending performances on television. He tried it himself, and was able to bend spoons. He then wanted to find a theory that would clarify the phenomenon. An idea of electromagnetic mechanics with complex numbers flashed upon him suddenly while he was enjoying a cup of saké on New Year's Day in 1983. The theory occurred to him largely complete. When I met Inomata, I tried to sense his *qi* with my intuitional *qi*. He had very strong *qi* energy, as I had expected. He also had an outstanding ability to receive *qi*. Intuitional flashes during relaxation after intensive study occur frequently to people like him.

Free Energy and Vacuums

Pantheistic "consciousness" is defined as non-physical energy, or so-called "free energy," which corresponds to physical energy. It means that even vacuums, in which nothing physical exists, are not empty space. On the contrary, space is full of "free energy." Inomata's theory suggests the possibility that a special technique could extract "free energy" and change it into electric energy. In Japan and several other countries, a machine called the N-machine is being used to extract "free energy," producing more than ten times the amount of electricity originally input. With this, various academic groups have finally begun to recognize the concept of free energy. Acceptance of this concept would be an incredible thing. It would demand that we change our entire outlook on the universe. The world's oil resources are limited, and relying on nuclear power would pose a great danger to the environment. The need for renewable, safe, and inexpensive sources of energy is pressing. Thus, free energy gives us reason to hope for the future.

The View of Existence in Inomata's Theory

Inomata's theory holds that there are levels of consciousness in minerals, plants, animals, and human beings (Figure 17–2). Although most minerals consist mainly of matter, a sacred stone worshipped religiously, or a precious stone maintained with a great deal of care may have consciousness, for *qi* information is registered in it. It also has energy, as it can be burned or combined. Plants have metabolism; they photosynthesize and react electrically to stimula, and they exchange information with one another, using an aromatic substance called photonchid. They have energy, and it can be said that they have consciousness on a certain level. Animals obviously exist with consciousness, a physical body and energy.

How about human beings? The amount of conscious energy differs from one person to another. No other creatures are like that. Plants or animals generally show very little difference, within a species, in the level of their conscious activity. But human beings do show tremendous variation in the degree of their conscious activity. The people whom we call "geniuses" usually have markably advanced levels of conscious activity. For example, the great astrophysicist Stephen Hawking, has conscious energy far beyond the common understanding of medicine.

I often think about the reason why we are born into this world. After studying *qi* for many years, I have come to believe that we enter this world in order to develop our consciousness. Once we recognize the existence of *qi* and are able to use *qi* well, we become able to control our bodies. Furthermore, when we reach the stage of being able to use conscious energy, we become aware of our intuitional ability and our creativity. At that point, the evolution of consciousness becomes a significant theme in our life, no matter what our occupation or our position in society may be.

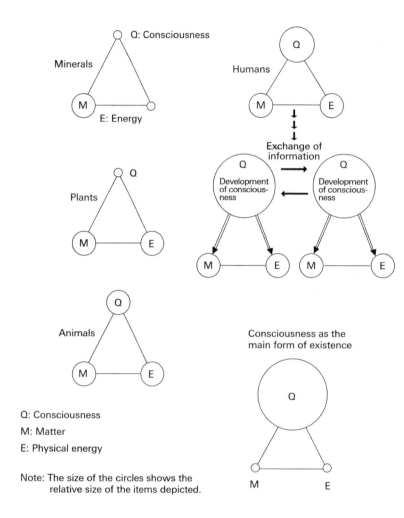

Figure 17–2
The form of existence of all things and beings, according to Inomata.

When your conscious energy expands to a certain degree, you will naturally begin to notice that human beings are constantly exchanging information without the use of any words. When your intuitive recognition develops, you may find that you no longer feel resistance toward acknowledging the existence of pure consciousness. Consciousness at this level probably corresponds to what people called "spirits" or "gods" in ancient times. But, as Figure 17–2 shows, existence at this level has very little physical energy, which means that it cannot be measured physically, and cannot be included in scientific discussions. Some people speak enthusiastically about this level of their experience, but in fact it is not necessary, and it is often not advisable, to speak freely about experience of this sort.

Creation Inseparable from Vibration

If we were to consider Inomata's theory for a moment as the basic theory of *qigong*, what conclusions would be draw? Surely one conclusion would be that existence is a form of creation, and creation is inseparable from vibration. Another would be that creation exists with vibration. Physical energy (E) has vibration, which takes the form, for instance, of electromagnetic waves or electric power waves. Matter has vibration at the level of atoms or elementary particles. At the atomic level, material consists of particles and vibrations; this idea is the basis of quantum physics. Does consciousness have vibration? When your sense of *qi* has improved, you will know that *qi* has various characteristics: it can be soft, rough, cold, warm, soothing, disturbing, etc. Music can move us when the players send us their conscious energy through the sound. Brain wave activity appears as a result of conscious activity. I believe that vibration is a natural element in consciousness too. Matter at its most basic level consists of vibration, just as does consciousness.

In the future, a method for converting the vibration of consciousness into electric energy might be developed. Today we can say at least that consciousness has a characteristic of vibration at the level of sensation. Matter, physical energy, and consciousness have a character of vibration, so it seems to be possible to formulate as a basic theory of the *qigong* method the idea that "Creation has vibration." We can make practical use of this theory in our lives; if we can freely create vibration of consciousness, we will also be able to freely control consciousness, matter, and physical energy. I mentioned earlier that Inomata's theory could be explained because of the belief that vibration of consciousness makes possible various paranormal phenomena, such as psychokinesis, ESP, and telepathy.

The Origin of Creation

The phenomena that can be achieved as a result of greater consciousness are not limited to the paranormal. You may have heard successful people say that they always thought positively, or that they had visualized their achievements as already having been accomplished. Vibration or energy of consciousness seems to act on us and form our society. But most people are not aware of this, because the results of positive thinking do not appear immediately, while paranormal phenomena can be manifested in a short time. Human beings can handle matter and energy freely in the dimension of dreams. Small children spend as much as fifty percent of their time in this dimension. While they grow, they are forced to learn the rules of the physical world with its many restrictions, and the idea that the physical world is the dominant reality is imprinted in their common consciousness.

But imagine for a moment a new era when people recognize that the energy of all consciousness is the origin of creation. Surely this would help increase the amount of harmony and well-being in the world. Since healing with mind energy would be accepted practice, the incidence of disease would decrease. The growing popularity of *qigong* speaks well for the harmonious currents of the world.

Message from a Psychic Performance

Toshihide Hisamura, whom I introduced as a psychic in the preceding chapter, gives concrete form to Inomata's theory. His performance is, one might say, the tangible expression of Inomata's theory. Hisamura has highly developed psychic abilities. He has at his disposal extraordinary paranormal abilities and he demonstrates his powers easily and without exhaustion. As I mentioned before, he can make objects float, bend spoons by throwing them into the air, change a spoon into a fork merely by holding it in his hand, use psychographics, ESP, and many other psychic phenomena. Most people are so astonished that they cannot believe their own eyes. Furthermore, he can repeat his performance as many times as he is requested. Psychic people usually limit the number of their performances, for fear that they will not always achieve the same results. They are often exhausted after a performance. Hisamura's "real job," however, is operating a small coffee shop, where he performs for about an hour, two or three times, after all his customers have finished eating. He does not stand on ceremony or demand authority as a result of his psychic power. He does not charge for people to see his performances. The only requirement he makes is that customers order something from the menu, like a soft drink or a plate of rice curry. He makes a living on the income from this small coffee shop, where he works very hard all day preparing the food he will serve that night. You might wonder why Mr. Hisamura does his psychic performances this way, after cooking all day in his shop. He could probably become well known and wealthy if he were to publicize his ability. I have heard some people remark, while watching his performances, that they would try to make a fortune in the lottery or at the racetrack, or perhaps control other people's minds, if they had Hisamura's psychic power. But I know that Hisamura simply does not want to use his abilities to avoid any of the demands or rigors of ordinary life.

I think Hisamura's performance sends us a silent message. When I observed him closely, I could sense his energy of consciousness as vibration, and the barricade of my own subconscious began to diminish gradually. Every time I have met him, I have been impressed over again with the mind's endless, untapped potential.

You may also have heard of Saibaba, from India. He materializes jewels, watches, etc. from empty space. People who have met him say that he has all kinds of psychic power. In Japan, there are several people I know personally, who can materialize things from space. Unlike Saibaba, they are quite ordinary people, and are willing to demonstrate their psychic performance for me. Seeing them always makes me feel as if human beings are actually *meant* to have limitless abilities.

XVIII — Memory and Location

Vibration of Mind Energy

The idea of a location's having memory may sound strange to you, but it is important to consider that a place may be deeply influenced by the deeds of people who lived there in the past or who live there today.

Apparently, modern science has no room for this kind of thinking, and of course intuitive investigations of this sort does not allow for the kind of replicability or measurability of results that would make them acceptable to modern science. In *Psychics and Mysteries*, written by Collin Wilson, you can learn more about the concept of the "memory of a location" as advanced by the late Tom Lethbridge, who was an archaeologist at Cambridge University. Lethbridge advocated the "tape recorder" theory after devoting himself to research on dowsing with pendulums (also known as radiesthesia). According to his theory, conscious energy can be carved as vibrations into the objects that surround us, and every existence has vibration. Lethbridge also believed that anyone can learn to sense these vibrations using a pendulum. For one of his experiments based on the "tape recorder" theory, he was able to use a forty-inch pendulum to measure the vibration in stones collected in a fortress that was built during the Iron Age. On the other hand, stones collected from a beach did not react to the pendulum at all. After he threw this second set of stones in anger, however, they did react. This led him to theorize that perhaps the stones in the fortress had once been thrown from a catapult in a fit of anger.

In addition, one day when he and his wife were collecting seaweed on the beach, they became unreasonably depressed. His wife was standing on a cliff, and she felt an overwhelming impulse to jump. Later, Lethbridge discovered that a man had leapt from that same cliff to his death. He came to the conclusion that the feelings of despair associated with suicide had been "carved" into the location—

that is, that the vibration of consciousness was "tape recorded" onto objects at the site of the suicide. Lethbridge, who had been a great archaeologist, devoted his life after retirement to research into the pendulum and dowsing, because he was so impressed by the consistency and replicability of the results of testing with a pendulum. He assumed that pendulums react to various objects and thoughts whose vibration is measurable. Wilson admires Lethbridge, and so do I, because of my own experiences with pendulums.

Purifying a Site with Esoteric Buddhism

One of my friends has been practicing *qigong* for several years. He now has mastered the Macrocosmic Orbit method and is able to use external *qi*. When he decided to look for the piece of land on which to build a house, he first succeeded in finding a location with positive *qi*. A real estate agent then introduced him to a different piece of land, however, saying that it would be very convenient to school and shopping. But the second location somehow turned out to have negative *qi*, and the agent was honest enough to tell him that the location would require purification before the house could be built. The site was troubled by spirits, which several different faith healers had tried in vain to exorcise. When my friend saw the location, he could sense strong *qi* emanating from the large camphor trees. From the building site next door, he also sensed a tingling, like an angry vibration. He decided to buy the site because he was sure that he could purify it. When I visited the site, I had the same impression. We invited a high priest to come and conduct a purification ceremony. The priest had studied and practiced the asceticism of esoteric Buddhism. After the solemn ceremony, my friend and I both felt sure that the site's *qi* had been purified. Later, we happened to learn that there had formerly been a pond and a temple of Inari (the harvest god) next to the building site, and that a developer had unceremoniously bulldozed them.

By the way, you may be surprised by the idea of holding an esoteric Buddhist ceremony in order to purify a site's *qi*. But in fact, from the point of controlling mind energy, the *qigong* method and the way of esotericism have something in common as techniques for controlling *qi* energy. If we were to consciously modernize the *qi* techniques contained in the ancient tradition of esoteric Buddhism, it would be possible to develop a very interesting *qigong* method. A study that I have been conducting on the technique for controlling external *qi* with a vajra or with the ceremonial tools used in esoteric Buddhist ceremonies is now nearly complete. I have actually confirmed its effectiveness clinically, and delivered a lecture on this topic at a symposium on mysticism and science held in Beijing in 1990, at which Chinese *qigong* masters Li Zhao-Sheng and Yang Wen-Yen were present. Both these masters are experts in external *qi*. They taught me several mystic secret mudras, or symbolic hand gestures, which I will discuss in Chapter XIX.

The Qi Consensus Method

It is not easy to measure the *qi* of a location. You may wonder how it is even possible to verify that a location has been successfully purified. The *qi* consensus method is useful for this purpose. In this method, more than one person must judge a certain *qi* phenomenon independently, without discussing it previously. The judges are required to have a certain ability to recognize *qi*. No one person's judgment should be valued more highly than another's. This is the *qi* consensus method.

Interestingly enough, when I try this method with my *qi* friends, the rate of our agreement on basic recognition is extremely high. Furthermore, we notice things that we had not noticed before. Thus, we are able to draw conclusions that are reasonable. People who are not convinced by the *qi* consensus method have a tendency to lose themselves by following authority figures. These people insist that neither the invisible world nor any phenomena that have not yet been scientifically verified even exists, but as soon as they encounter some incomprehensible phenomena or unfortunate turns of event, they change their attitude totally and follow someone who seems at home in the invisible world.

The *qi* consensus method makes you maintain your unhampered reasoning, and at the same time it helps you to progress in your ability to recognize the invisible world. For this reason, it is important to have friends who practice *qi* with you. Friends with advanced *qi* ability can give you advice. This is important, because you will need to talk openly about *qi* with someone when you enter the *qi* world. It is also important to know an advanced practitioner who can advise you, especially when you cannot achieve consensus with others at your *qi* level. You also should know what kind of person would be an ideal adviser for you. The following are points to bear in mind when judging whether someone would make a good teacher:

1. He or she should neither make a show of authority, nor demand too much formality. Remember too that a license or certificate doesn't mean much.

2. Better teachers have less need to emphasize secrets or special talents. If an advisor requires trainees to have secrets

or special talents, this suggests that he or she is not capable of bringing *qigong* techniques taught into general usage and thus of making them useful to society.

3. An advisor must be someone whose life would be exemplary even if the *qi* component were not taken into consideration. If one depends only on *qi* ability, it is hard to live a useful life in the real world.

4. An advisor must be aware that *qigong* is not just a Chinese technique. An advisor should study various spiritual traditions from all over the world, including Shintoism and esoteric Buddhism; these traditions have a great deal to offer *qi* practice.

Distinguishing good and bad *qi* is not difficult: Inhale, visualizing that you are absorbing positive *qi* energy from certain things, people, places which release good *qi*. Try this with negative *qi* too. How do you feel? Does it not seem that you are able to inhale more energy with the positive *qi*?

This is one way to learn whether the *qi* energy of certain things or people is good or bad for you.

What Is Feng Shui?

Feng shui is a practical form of geomancy used in daily life in Taiwan, Hong Kong, and Okinawa (Japan's southern most island) even today. "Feng" means wind, and "shui" water in Chinese. It is a system of thought combined by the physiognomy of a house and a grave, the aspect of a piece of land as an environmental assessment, a theory of location like a city plan, gardens, and a theory of movement that suggests placement of furniture, where indoor plants should be placed, where the bathroom should be, and so on. After *qi* is judged by visible phenomena like wind, water, streets, etc., living space is rearranged so that positive *qi* ensues.

According to *feng shui*, there are three basic elements: mountains, water or rivers, and direction. The wind controls weather and climate, while water is a symbol of the earth that receives wind or *qi* from heaven. Wind is thought to be the master, and water the follower. While some places have strong vital energy, other places have weak energy. The ancients studied natural phenomena to improve their living conditions. You might have a brief idea by now that *feng shui* is a technique of understanding *qi* of the environment. In *feng shui* theory, a mountain is comparable to a dragon, and so a dragon range indicates a mountain range. Vital *qi* rises on the summit and flows down to a plain along ranges. Dragons jumping up and down are considered to be full of vibrant energy, while flat dragons have little to offer. A stony mountain without soil, a range that is cut off, and a mountain with no grass or trees are all called dead dragons. Figure 18–1 shows an ideal configuration. The right and left ridgelines in black from Mount Zu-Zong are the dragon ranges. The most vital energy gathers in "Bright Hall," which is equal to an acupuncture point by the navel of a human body. The resident there can enjoy the benevolent influence.

Mount Zu-Zong

"Xue"

Bright Hall

Inner range

Mount An

River

Outer range

Mount Chao

Figure 18–1
Ideal *feng shui* map.

Why do the dragon ranges produce vital power and gather at one point? As far as I know, there is no document available at this point in time that can satisfactorily answer this question. But here is my preliminary theory: Three factors which produce vital *qi* of mountain ranges are currents of underground water, currents of wind, and mountains that contain minerals that in turn produce *qi*. Figure 18–2 indicates two directions of *qi* flow from mountain ranges. One (on the right) is from mountain ranges that spiral in a clockwise direction, and the other (on the left) is from mountain ranges that spiral counterclockwise. The ranges look like dragons lying in a coil around the spot "Bright Hall." Rainwater that flows along the ranges forms veins of water underground that converge at the end to form rivers. I explained before that *qi* spirals clockwise. Figure 18–2 shows what I interpret as the vital energy of the ranges flowing in a way that is similar to the law of the right-handed screw from electromagnetism. In effect, the counterclockwise ranges let the *qi* of the earth gush out through the spot "Bright Hall," while the clockwise mountain ranges make cosmic *qi* flow over that same spot. Thus, I suppose that this spot turns into a very positive place.

Judging Qi Direction

The flow of water as the second basic element in *feng shui* can be thought of as the same as the underground water which forms a part of the mountain ranges. The concept of the spiral is basic when it comes to reading *qi* flow.

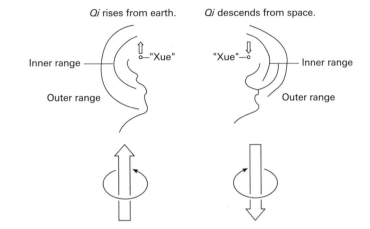

Figure 18–2
Feng shui and *qi*.

Direction is the third element in *feng shui*. *Feng shui* masters judge the *qi* of the earth with a compass (measuring device) called Le-Jing (Figure 18–3), combined with the five natural elements, eight signs of divination, twelve zodiac signs, twenty directions, twenty-eight polar stages along the zodiac, etc. These rules can seem extremely complicated, so I also formulated a tentative theory based on my intuition. Stand outside, facing in each of the four directions in turn, with a completely open *qi* sense. There are *qi* currents running from north to south and from east to west. You may notice that *qi* flows very smoothly from north to south. This might be caused by the magnetic field of the earth. I intuit—and friends of mine whose *qi* sense is advanced agree—that the rotation of the earth makes *qi* flow from east to west (Figure 18–4), although no one has ever actually proven this. At the moment there is no way to measure *qi* direction.

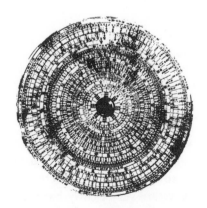

Figure 18–3
Feng shui measuring device (Le-Jing).

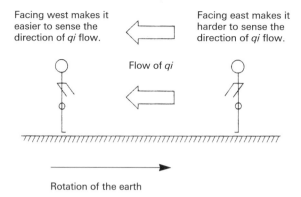

Facing west makes it easier to sense the direction of *qi* flow.

Facing east makes it harder to sense the direction of *qi* flow.

Flow of *qi*

Rotation of the earth

Figure 18–4
Sensing the direction of *qi* flow.

Try the following experiment with a friend who is able to use external *qi* to a certain degree. Facing each other, practice having one of you release *qi*, and the other receive it. You should be able to feel that it is easier to sense *qi* when it is sent from north to south and from east to west, than when it is sent from south to north or west to east. If you try combining the flows of *qi* from north to south and from east to west (Figure 18–5), the result will be a vector flow from northeastern part to southwest, and a smoother *qi* flow. Traditionally, the northeast is referred to as the "gateway of demons" in Japan, and this direction is thought to be full of impurities that must be avoided. The ancient people also guarded the northeastern part of any battlefield especially heavily. Maybe they could sense that *qi* flows from northeast to southwest.

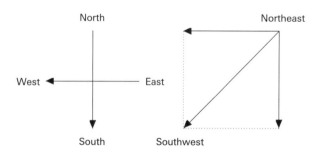

North

Northeast

West

East

South

Southwest

Figure 18–5

Electromagnetic Pollution

In *feng shui*, there are certain negative natural factors (such as *sakki*; literally, "murderous *qi*") that are thought to have a negative effect on *qi*. In the same way, some manmade structures such as high-voltage cables or even highways are very clearly hazardous to our health and well-being. These factors play an important role in the *qi* environment.

In particular, high-voltage cables disturb *qi* because of their strong electromagnetic fields. People have finally started to discuss this as a form of pollution. Under normal conditions, electromagnetic waves cannot be recognized despite the substantial threat that they pose to our health. It is reported that a larger number of traffic accidents occur near high-voltage cables than elsewhere. If you suffer from poor health and at the same time you use a machine that produces strong electromagnetic waves, or you live near high-voltage cables, it may be worth considering a change. Living near a highway does not seem to be healthy either. Industrial medicine has also begun to consider this subject. What you can do when looking for a place to live is to do your best to find a place that is in a natural setting and that has good *feng shui* conditions, while at the same time strengthening your own energy with *qigong* against negative *qi* from unpleasant factors in your environment. As another form of *qi* disturbance, it is also a good idea to consider the influence of people who affect you in a negative way. If human beings understand the environment's influence on *qi*, they should be able to live in greater harmony with one another and with industry.

XIX — Practical Thoughts on Qi Training

Questions and Answers

I would now like to address some questions I have been asked by readers of my books and articles and by people who are using my video to practice *qigong*.

Question: I have been practicing the Microcosmic Orbit method to straighten and strengthen my back. Now I hear that men and women's *qi* flows in opposite directions but that some men's *qi* flows in the female direction, and some women's flows in the male. I am a man, and I have been practicing the Microcosmic Orbit method assuming that my *qi* flows in the male direction. But my *qi* flow doesn't seem smooth, and I sometimes suspect that it might actually be of the female type. How can I find out which type I have?

Answer: If you put on the Cosmic Headband, you will know if the direction of your *qi* flow is male or female by doing the Reflection of *Qi* Muscle Power test. If your fingers are stronger when the metal badge is in the middle of your forehead, and weaker when the badge is at the back of your head, your *qi* flows in the direction customary for your sex. But if your fingers are weaker when the badge is in the middle of your forehead and stronger when the metal badge is at the back of your head, your *qi* flows in the direction customary for the opposite sex.

If you do not have a Cosmic Headband, observe your breathing carefully while making what is known as the Microcosmic Orbit mudra. Place your hands close together, your palms facing, and your right hand above the left hand. Form rings with the middle finger and thumb of both hands. Then connect the rings like a chain and put all the other fingers into the circles (Figure 19–1). When the right hand is over the left hand, *qi* flow in the male direction is promoted. When the left hand is over the right hand, *qi* flow in the female direction is promoted. Try it both ways, and you will notice which arrangement of the hands allows you to breathe more comfortably. After Master Li Zhao-Sheng introduced me to this mudra, I found that it can change the direction of *qi* flow. It seems to function as a "switch" with which *qi* direction can be changed. This method is very effective for ascertaining the direction of one's *qi* flow; forty-five out of fifty patients who are sensitive to *qi* can recognize the change of breathing by making the mudra. In addition, this method is useful when you practice the Microcosmic Orbit method without making a *qi* ball, and with visualization alone.

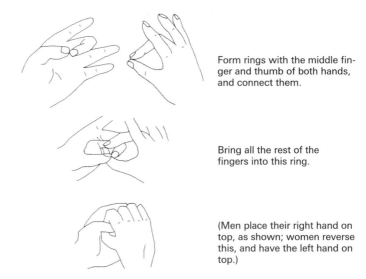

Figure 19–1
Mudra of the Micro-
cosmic Orbit.

Form rings with the middle finger and thumb of both hands, and connect them.

Bring all the rest of the fingers into this ring.

(Men place their right hand on top, as shown; women reverse this, and have the left hand on top.)

It is rare, but there are people who are not affected at all by the Cosmic Headband. These people generally fall into two categories: those whose *qi* is too blocked to react, and those whose *qi* energy is extremely high and therefore is not affected by the magnetic stimulus of the Cosmic Headband. Those with blocked *qi* do not recognize a difference in their breathing when they make the mudra, and many of them suffer from headaches caused by stress and stiffness in the neck or shoulders. If you do not feel a change in your breathing, you should continue practicing the basic *qigong* of the Microcosmic Orbit method that is intended to strengthen your backbone, because the *qi* within you is not active enough to control the energy of the Microcosmic Orbit. This exercise is also important because it can help you to avoid suffering any side effects as a result of doing the Microcosmic Orbit method.

Question: Since I started practicing the Microcosmic Orbit method with a *qi* ball, I have been having difficulty falling asleep, and I feel almost as if something is flowing constantly through my body. Also, a painful injury I had a long time ago has started bothering me again. I feel almost feverish, and have headaches.

Answer: You are probably not practicing the basic *qigong* of the Microcosmic Orbit method which I systematized for straightening and strengthening the backbone. Most people who have the symptoms that you describe are not practicing the exercise properly, or are allowing their *qi* to circulate in the wrong direction. The energy of the Microcosmic Orbit method protects us from illness and keeps us healthy, but since it is deeply interrelated with the body its flow can be disturbed by any imbalance or distortion within the body. When *qi* is blocked, it is necessary to perform basic *qigong* of the Microcosmic Orbit method, which involves swinging the backbone either back and forth or from side to side, or doing the "bear" movement. In the past, before I had become aware of the basic *qigong* method, two or three cases patients of mine experienced these same side effects. But since I introduced my method of basic *qigong* exercise, which can be practiced using videos, these problems have disappeared.

Another way to avoid side effects is to completely open the downward *qi* flow. When *qi* energy increases, *qi* tends to move upward by itself. Therefore, if the upward flow is promoted too much by the use of a *qi* ball, *qi* may collect in the head, causing headaches, irritability, or hot flashes.

Question: I have been practicing the Microcosmic Orbit method every day for six months, and I finally sense the flow of *qi* in my body. I had been suffering from a weak stomach for a long time, but I am well now and don't tire so easily. Recently, though, my *qi* flow changed direction. I had a male type before and now I have a female type. Can you explain how this could happen?

Answer: Let me tell you about my own experience. When I mastered the Microcosmic Orbit method, my Chakras opened. As soon as I mastered the Macrocosmic Orbit method, I became able to control the direction of *qi* flow. This same thing also happened to all my patients who practiced *qigong*. A couple of years ago, I was invited to a meeting of a *qigong* group, where I spoke about the Microcosmic Orbit method. One young man said that he had been training in the martial arts and *qigong* for many years in China. He said that my theory on the different direction of *qi* flow in men and women was not to be found anywhere in the Chinese classical documents, and that his master had never mentioned such a thing. I told him that it was my own hypothesis and that I had been researching it clinically with ultrasound, thermography, and the AMI machine (which measures the energy of meridians). So although this idea may sometimes be criticized, more and more people are beginning to accept it. A member of a Taoist sect once sent me a document that discusses this difference in *qi* flow direction between men and women.

When I first introduced my *qigong* method, most people were not familiar with even the phrase "Microcosmic Orbit." Naturally, my theory that *qi* flow could change direction during *qigong* training sessions must have sounded quite strange to people at that time. That's why I waited for a while, until the time was right, to present it. Today we can talk openly with *qigong* practitioners about the direction of *qi* flow. People's understanding of *qigong* has greatly deepened in recent years.

Master Tang Wei-Zhong, who came to Japan to teach Buddhist *qigong*, once told me that he often practiced making his *qi* flow in both directions. He also demonstrated this ability to me.

To summarize my thoughts, I would say that the direction of our *qi* flow is fixed in the stage of the Microcosmic Orbit, but when our skill progresses beyond that, the direction can reverse. But *qi* flow seems to revert to its original direction after the new *qi* flow has developed to a certain level. When the Chakras are all open and you have mastered the Macrocosmic Orbit, you will also be able to control the direction of *qi* flow. This means that after you can control the direction of *qi* flow in the Microcosmic Orbit method, your Chakras will open and you will then be able to say that you have mastered the Macrocosmic Orbit method. If you can control the direction of *qi* flow, this means that you are a "hermaphrodite" in terms of *qi*. By this I mean that you have achieved a combination of maternal and paternal elements, or a balance between yin and yang. When men try to make their *qi* flow in the direction of a woman's, or a woman tries to make her *qi* circulate in the male direction, they gain access to feelings and emotions that they have never experienced before.

Question: I work as an acupuncturist. Having mastered the Macrocosmic Orbit method, I am able to absorb *qi* from earth and space through Xien-Gu and Gai-Hui, and I can release external *qi* from Lao-Gong of my hands. Mastering this method has greatly improved my skill as an acupuncturist. I do not receive negative *qi* from patients, and I do not become exhausted very quickly. But when I work hard with patients who have difficult diseases, I do still get tired. Do you think I will ever reach a level at which I will not experience exhaustion?

Answer: I am sometimes asked this same question by osteopaths who use external *qi* when treating patients. As a general rule, using more than one's limit does produce fatigue. But you must have noticed that you recover from your fatigue much more quickly now than when you were working at the level of the Microcosmic Orbit. You should also find that after you recover from the fatigue, your ability to release external *qi* has improved. Your ability to release external *qi* actually develops by repeating this process. Gradually you will come to understand that you are not using your own *qi* energy, but that you are transmitting *qi* to patients from earth and space.

External *qi* is useful for medical practitioners, who often have many opportunities to use it. But I think that training primarily for the purpose of releasing external *qi* is unnecessary for ordinary people. You can use your *qi* ability to increase your creativity and expand your potential. It is a waste to limit *qi* ability to medical purposes. *Qi* energy is a well-spring of mental activity. You can enjoy it in many different ways.

The chart in Figure 19–2 brings together many of the things that I have mentioned in this chapter. It can serve as a "map and a compass" for the traveller through the world of *qi*. Refer to it occasionally to get a sense of exactly where you are.

Qi level	Activated *qi* through the 12 meridians	Microcosmic Orbit	Microcosmic Orbit	Transcendental Orbit
Qi channel	12 meridians	Du-Mai, Ren-Mai	Ren-Mai, Du-Mai, Chong-Mai, Dai-Mai	The entire body
Purpose	Clearing *qi* blockages, healing oneself	Increasing energy, promoting one's own health	Becoming better able to input/output *qi* information	Achieving oneness with the universe
Distinctive character	Movement of hands and feet, many restrictions	Straightening the backbone, controlling *qi* with the *qi* ball	Clearing Chakras by absorbing *qi* from earth and space	OM *qigong*
Diagnosing ability (the "compass")	—	Wearing the Cosmic Headband backward, doing the Reflection of *Qi* Muscle Power test	Diagnosing Chakra level with the Macrocosmic Ring, 3-pronged and 5-pronged vajras, and the Reflection of *Qi* Muscle Power test	No need
Self-awareness	Physical experience of the *qi* sense	Awareness of the energy field that surrounds human beings	Exchange between the Macrocosmos and Microcosmos	Higher than previous level
Illnesses that can be healed	Functional disorders	Ordinary pain and functional disorders	Difficult diseases and mental disorders	Higher than previous level
External *qi*	Exhaustion when releasing *qi*, low energy	Still exhausted when releasing *qi*, restrictions based on distance	No exhaustion when releasing *qi*, no restrictions based on distance	Higher than previous level
Number of patients at a time	—	One patient	Many patients	Higher than previous level
Brain waves	—	Alpha	Beta and theta	Theta only

Figure 19–2
Map and compass for the traveller through the world of *qi*.

Danger and Pitfalls

There is one important thing that advanced *qi* practitioners must bear in mind. There is nothing wrong with feeling joy at one's accomplishments, but believing that you are the best or looking down on others is very dangerous. The moment that you start too think you are the best, you shut off the way to further progress. When people know that you have advanced *qi* ability, they will be drawn to you, and you will feel comfortable with them. For some period of time you may well be the center of attention in the group. But that's exactly when you should bear in mind that there is still progress that you need to make.

I will mention a case here that I am familiar with personally. There was a man who was known as a master of external *qi*. He had been sick for a long time, but during his recuperation, he became aware of cosmic energy and eventually healed himself. No one taught him how to use external *qi*, yet he also learned to heal others. As time went on he healed a great many people. Through intensive training, he also learned to use his intuition very effectively, and was good at sensing other people's *qi* ability. Then the problems began. He started to criticize and belittle other *qigong* and Yoga masters. Some of the things he said sounded reasonable enough, and people around him agreed with him. After a while, he became convinced of his own greatness, even claiming that he was a reincarnation of an earlier great master. I regret to say that he completely wasted his ability.

In order to avoid a "master" complex, you must understand that you will always be in a process of evolution. No matter how high a level of *qi* ability you achieve, you will never reach the goal or attain perfection.

Some may feel that they want *qi* ability because it will enable them to dominate others. This is a common pitfall among people who train in the use of *qi*. I admit that it is possible to use *qi* ability in a negative way, just as it is to attack someone with *qi*. Someone might succeed in dominating others this way, but his or her evolution will stop as a result. Some people feel that they can establish their own power only by dominating and gaining authority over others. This is a reflection of an inner weakness of which they are unaware. If you have mastered the Macrocosmic Orbit method and will know that you are constantly receiving external *qi* from earth and space, you will realize the true meaning of power and know that dominating others is meaningless. To avoid some of the common pitfalls encountered by people involved in the study of spiritual things, simply stand close to nature and be thankful that you are alive. Allow nature's love to enter you. Once you recognize that you are a part of the universe, you will not long to dominate others.

Washing Negative Qi Away

In the world of *qi*, human beings are still in the primitive stage, like babies who often stumble and fall when they start to walk. As you continue to practice *qigong*, you may see psychological and physical changes. As long as you are practicing the Microcosmic Orbit method properly, no particular change will occur. But when you begin to realize that you are communicating with the *qi* of the universe, you will start to change. Don't be afraid of this change, because it is a form of evolution. You will come to understand that you are more than your physical body and that human beings exchange *qi* energy constantly with all other forms of existence. In this respect, proper training in absorbing and releasing external *qi* is necessary. Money and material goods may decrease with use, but external *qi* does not. You can obtain as much external *qi* as you want. The best way to realize that *qi* is limitless is to rid yourself of all egoism.

Dozens of my former patients have been practicing the Microcosmic and Macrocosmic Orbit methods for several years and have now learned to release external *qi*, although at first their *qi* energy was weaker than most people's. They come to see me for advice only when they run into a problem. Often they complain of "crooked *qi*" caused by releasing *qi* to heal people suffering from difficult diseases. I always praise them for having this complaint. They look puzzled at first. But when they realize that this kind of difficulty is a normal step in the process of their evolution, the problem is half solved. If they still complain about a troubled *qi* flow, I will correct it, but often they learn quickly how to resolve the problem themselves.

If you feel that you have received negative *qi*, hold your hands under running water and imagine that you are washing negative *qi* away. This is an easy way to solve various *qi*-related problems. If you need more powerful effects, take a shower, again using your imagination in this same way. Japanese people have traditionally poured cold water over themselves or stood under waterfalls as a spiritual and ascetic exercise. Maybe we should pay more attention to traditional methods of cleansing *qi*. However, it is also important to remember that healing patients is not an essential part of the training to use external *qi*. Everyone has self-healing power. When you try to heal patients, you are simply activating their self-healing power. Your power to heal should be considered nothing more than getting patients warmed up. Making patients depend on your healing power is not recommended.

"Double Computers"

Having "double computers"—one of the *qi* world, one of reality—allows you to be inventive. Assuming that these two computers are fully linked to one another, you will find it easy to understand the *qi* world theoretically, and will be able to input information in the form of concrete suggestions for your "computer of the *qi* world" about the next step it should perform. People whose "computer of the real world" is functioning well usually show good common sense as well as respect for social rules. They are capable of leading an exemplary life even without the power of *qi* (Figure 19–3).

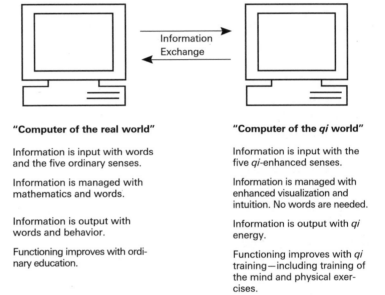

"Computer of the real world"

Information is input with words and the five ordinary senses.

Information is managed with mathematics and words.

Information is output with words and behavior.

Functioning improves with ordinary education.

"Computer of the *qi* world"

Information is input with the five *qi*-enhanced senses.

Information is managed with enhanced visualization and intuition. No words are needed.

Information is output with *qi* energy.

Functioning improves with *qi* training—including training of the mind and physical exercises.

NOTE: Our skills and abilities—particularly our sensory perception and creativity—improve greatly when we merge these two computers.

Figure 19–3
Features of the two "computers."

In fact, it is possible to attain ability in the invisible world relatively quickly. The way to do this is simply to shut out the computer of the real world. This method has been practiced by religeous ascetics since ancient times. Ascetic practitioners often lead a life of seclusion in order to avoid inputting any information from the visible world. Under these circumstances, the computer of the *qi* world is liable to start working regardless of whether a practitioner is ready to use it. Illusions and auditory hallucinations often occur to people who undertake such practice. An ascetic may sometimes get correct information about the invisible world, but if the checks and balances offered by the computer of the real world are not in place, the ascetic's approach can sometimes become fanatical.

You always need to remain aware. If you seek greater spiritual health, keep both your "computers" in good condition. If both are functioning well, you should find yourself feeling extremely creative and inventive. Formulate hypotheses from your intuitions, and then confirm them with the computer of the real world. This approach helped me to invent the Cosmic Headband, an ultrasound machine for the Microcosmic Orbit, and a ceramic vajra. I also used it in conceiving the theory of the opposite *qi* flow in men and women.

The World Is Full of Mysteries

Prior to the development of modern science, human beings shared a common idea about the structure of the world. Phenomena that lay beyond the possibility of comprehension with the five senses were entrusted to people who showed paranormal abilities. People believed in supernatural phenomena, and thus religions evolved. Now, science illuminates the wonders of the world, and people set out to discover the material bounds or the beginning of the universe.

Measuring machines have been helping to extend and magnify human beings' limited sensory perception. At the same time, however, the use of the five senses has determined certain limits to modern science. We can see microscopic objects with an electron microscope or a cyclotron, and can perceive objects in distant parts of the universe with a radio telescope. But we must bear in mind that these measuring devices simply serve to magnify our sense of sight. When science was first developed and modern technology began to make life easier, people must have imagined that the power of science was unlimited. In the West, there was a time when some thinkers dared to proclaim that God was "dead." There seemed to be no mystery or source of wonder left in the world. But today we have begun to doubt the idea that science is everything, and have become more keenly aware of the contradictions inherent in modern science and technology. Faced with large-scale destruction of the environment and disregard for humanity, we are now questioning the idea that science can or should conquer nature. People have begun to think that there might be entire realms of experience that science is not equipped to explain.

Do not hesitate to trust your intuition and to think that something might be possible in the *qi* world. The way that you discover new knowledge is by hypothesizing your intuitions. What I call "structural hypothesizing" is a process of investigating what you do not know by developing a hypothesis about an idea that strikes you as plausible, then experimenting with it, practicing it, and asking others to try it. This is a very basic approach to knowledge, and it is often very exciting.

Don't worry if people have not yet been able to answer the questions you are asking. Your body knows the answers. When you discover something that is true, you should feel comfortable. Every experience that you have is a precious opportunity to further develop your *qi* ability. To do this you will simply need to use and to trust your ability to intuit which of several alternatives may be closest to the truth.

Yukio Funai of the Funai Institute gives us a standard for distinguishing things that are true from things that are false. He says that true things must be simple and clear, easy to practice, highly effective, effective with many things, and free from any side effects. I would like to add two more conditions to his list: things that are true make you feel more comfortable and also make you feel freer. Think of these seven conditions whenever you have difficulty deciding on or selecting something. These conditions apply not only to the *qi* world, but to many other things as well.

The *qigong* method is very effective as a practical way to train and develop our intuition and our ability to do structural hypothesizing. This keeps the mind from being limited by either logic or the five senses. I believe that the coming age will belong to people who have "double computers."

PART THREE
The Ultimate Reality

XX — Transpersonal Psychology

The Freedom Principle and Independence from Authority

Freedom in *qigong* differs qualitatively from external forms of freedom such as freedom of speech, freedom of religion, or freedom to choose one's political affiliation. *Qigong* requires complete inner freedom. The less restrictions a *qigong* method places on a trainee's thinking, the more advanced it is. Certificates from authorities are not needed as a proof of your expertise. Once you master the Macrocosmic Orbit method, your "computer of the *qi* world" begins to function, and you can communicate with people through the *qi* "network." When my patients ask me how many times they must repeat one movement, or whether they must practice *qigong* every day, I emphasize that there are no "musts," and no rules that apply to everyone. What is most important in *qigong* exercise is to listen to your body. In my *qigong* method, movement of the spine is important. Included in this are swinging the spine back and forth and to the right and left, twisting it, and tracing a figure-eight shape with it. If the backbone becomes straighter because of these movements, patients will have discovered the proper posture for Standing Zen. When patients tire quickly and are too weak to maintain one posture for any length of time, it is difficult for them to distribute strength to certain parts of the body or to hold the spine or neck completely straight. Naturally it is also difficult for them to perform Standing Zen, in which the legs firmly support the body while the arms are held out loosely and limply. Allowing the backbone to remain curved and weak makes it more difficult to become healthy. Patients whose spine is curved and weak generally also have weak muscles, and are easily tired. I show them the posture and style of movement that are best suited to the *qigong* method, but also I tell them to take it easy and to exercise at their own pace. Performing the *qigong* method with the kind of movements that are most comfortable for you is part of the principle of freedom.

Transpersonal Psychology

The theory of the subconscious as formulated by Freud is familiar to most people today. During meditation, when the mind is in a state of deep relaxation, thoughts and images rise to the surface from the subconscious, allowing "awareness" to take place. Throughout my career I have continued to study Freud's theories of the subconscious, Jung's collective unconscious, and works in transpersonal psychology by Ken Wilber and Stanislav Grof. I believe that *qigong* training involves much more than just becoming physically healthy. It is an effective method to pursue the question that is so central to transpersonal psychology, "*Who am I.*" To my way of thinking, the study of transpersonal psychology is essentially the study of the exchange of *qi*. When you realize that *qi* is present everywhere—not only within yourself and everyone else, but also within many other life forms—and that you can understand other beings more profoundly by exchanging *qi* with them, you are likely to find the field of transpersonal psychology very interesting.

The Spectrum of Consciousness Within Qigong

In his book *No Boundary*, Ken Wilber offers his concept of the "centaur level": "A centaur is a legendary animal, half human and half horse. It represents a perfect union of mental and physical harmony. A centaur is not a horse rider in control of his horse, but a rider who is one with his horse. It is not the psyche divorced from and in control of a soma, but a self-controlling, self-governing, psychosomatic unity." I would like to reconsider this concept in the context of the *qigong* method. When you practice Standing Zen or the Microcosmic Orbit method, you may lose all sensation in your trunk, legs, and hands, and feel as if you were melting away. Or you might feel as if you were standing in a hot tub with the water up to your neck. I call this condition the "melting sensation." At this point, you can gradually change an involuntary function to a voluntary one by controlling the flow of your *qi*. With this, your breathing will slow and deepen, your pulse will slow, and you will be easily able to release alpha waves continuously with brain wave biofeedback.

Wilber mentions the breathing method and muscle relaxation as methods of reaching the centaur level; however, it seems that the idea of controlling *qi* remains beyond the reach of his thought. In *qigong,* the centaur level can be explained as a state of stillness achieved with Standing Zen or the Microcosmic Orbit method. As for the concept of the "spectrum of consciousness," Wilber thoroughly studied various methodologies of the West and the East, including psychoanalysis, Zen, Bioenergetics, Gestalt, Transcendental Meditation, existentialism, and Hinduism. Although these systems of thought contradict one another, they are similarly important within the evolutionary current of consciousness (Figure 20–1). Wilber speaks of three major influences on world consciousness: the first is orthodox egoic psychology, including cognitive behaviorism and Freudian ego psychology; the second is traditions of humanistic psychology such as bioenergetics and Gestalt; the third is various forms of transpersonal psychology such as psychosynthesis, Jungian psychology, and the mystic traditions in general. Wilber systematized and generalized, indicating that various psychologies and methodologies are useful up to a certain stage. His work can be seen as a cartographic, or mandalic, concept. Whenever I read his work, I can't help but admire the logical and linguistic ability of Westerners. On the other hand, however, I have the impression that Orientals are better able to systematize and practice the training than Westerners. My intuition tells me that the practice of the Microcosmic and Macrocosmic Orbit methods is a system for the rapid evolution of consciousness, which has transpersonal psychology as one of its theoretical bases.

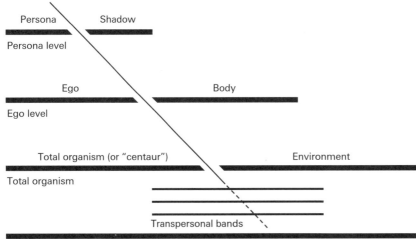

Figure 20–1
The spectrum of consciousness.

Lao-Tzu and Ken Wilber

When Ken Wilber was a junior at Duke University, he happened to read *Tao Te Ching* by Lao-Tzu, and his world view began to change fundamentally.

The Way that can be told of is not an Unvarying Way;
The names that can be named are not unvarying names.
It was from the Nameless that Heaven and Earth sprang;
The named is but the mother that rears the ten thousand
    creatures, each after its kind.

These are the opening lines of *Tao Te Ching*. After Wilber read this book, he went on to read all kinds of great books, Eastern and Western, on the meaning of life and the pursuit of happiness. I find it interesting that one young American student was so impressed that his world view changed completely. Perhaps he received a message from Lao-Tzu, suggesting that he should approach even his own thoughts with a measure of skepticism. In any case, his long journey to higher consciousness began with this book. But soon he found that his reading was only confusing him, because the ideas the books contained were so often contradictory. While Freudian ego psychology maintained that the strength of the ego was a barometer of mental health, for Buddhists, non-ego was the ideal state. Cognitive behaviorism saw answers hidden in a lifetime of learning and conditioning. On the other hand, Gestalt psychology emphasized the "here and now." Wilber was driven by a desire to organize these theories and doctrines, and to reconcile their apparent contradictions. Two ideas that would become representative of his thought were the spectrum of consciousness and the transcendental unity of religions. It is clear from his books that these two concepts are based in Wilber's Zen training and his experiences with Gestalt therapy.

The Ocean of Unity Consciousness

I would like to discuss Figure 20–2 by again referring to Wilber's *No Boundary*. I have added three elements to his original figure. These are the Microcosmic Orbit method, the Macrocosmic Orbit method and the "Transcendental level in *qigong*." The "persona" is a facet—a face adjusted to a society—while the "shadow" refers to a hidden desire. When the two are separated by a boundary, they struggle regularly. Then various symptoms and inconveniences occur which are treated with counseling and support therapy. The next level, in which the gap between the ego *per se* and the body is healed, is the level of the total organism—that is, the centaur level. This is equivalent to the stage of mastery of the Microcosmic Orbit method, at which time you can circulate *qi* through the body. Going deeper, the gap between the total organism and the environment is healed, resulting in a stage where the aim is to become one with the entire universe, or to form a harmonious whole of the self and not-self, attaining unity consciousness.

There are various forms of therapies and training for this stage. There are the transpersonal bands of the spectrum between the level of unity consciousness and the level of the total organism. The Macrocosmic Orbit method that connects you with external *qi* is like a form of training for the transpersonal bands of the spectrum. The transcendental level in *qigong* is beyond the level of the Macrocosmic Orbit, and equivalent to the condition of unity consciousness. According to Wilber, all esoteric truths—whether they be taught by Jesus Christ, the Buddha, or even physicist Erwin Schroedinger—are the same in terms of their "transcendental unity." These teachers all reached this level, recognized the same reality, and spoke from "religious" experiences. Variety arose from differences in their social and cultural backgrounds.

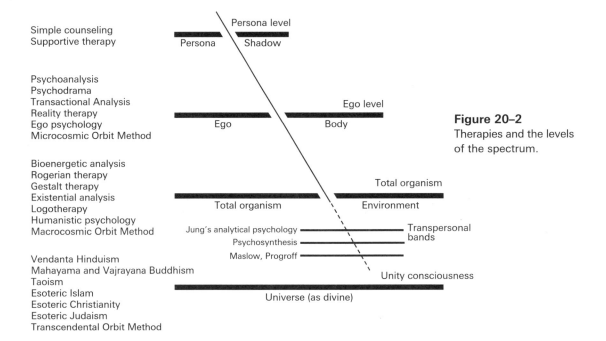

Figure 20–2
Therapies and the levels of the spectrum.

If you are able to perceive the transcendental unity of religion you should not have any trouble choosing from among various forms of training. You will likely also have a deep sympathy toward training methods other than your own. Finally, you will have a good sense of where you are and where you are heading when you practice. This will help you to remain positive about moving forward toward increased consciousness, despite any hardships that you may experience in reality (Figure 20–3). In *qigong*, you can speed your progress by remaining conscious of the stage to which you belong, the purpose of your training, and your goals.

People have different goals, even while undertaking the same training. Perhaps you wish to recover from illness, or to heal patients with external *qi*. Or your goal may be exchanging your *qi* with that of earth and space. Perhaps you would like to develop your consciousness by awakening your hidden talents. No matter what your goal may be, everything is flowing like one huge river into the ocean of unity consciousness, forming one harmonious whole of the self and not-self, just as Wilber described. In my opinion, if more people were convinced of the truth of unity consciousness, conflicts between individuals and also between larger groups could be greatly reduced.

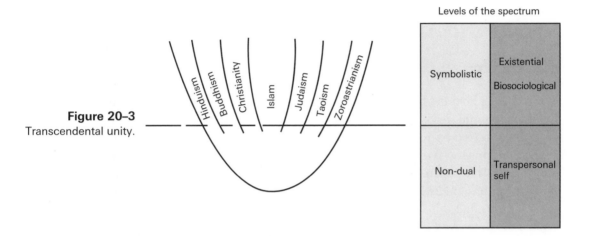

Figure 20–3
Transcendental unity.

When my *qi* friends and patients ask me if they are free to study other *qigong* methods as well, I tell them that they are free to study anything they please. I advise them simply to be aware of the stage to which their consciousness has progressed and the meaning of the things they are learning. We all have a certain sense of partisanship, and like to think that the approach wee have chosen is the best. But this kind of thinking can hold us back. I think we are very fortunate, in this modern age, to have Wilber's theory of the spectrum of consciousness. It would have been unthinkable for anyone to discover this sort of theory in the past, but the quality and quantity of information available in the modern world has made it possible. Today, one can learn *qigong* at home with books or videos. It is time that we also began to utilize the idea of the spectrum of consciousness, because this can lead us to the stage of freedom from restrictions—that is, true inner freedom.

XXI — The Evolution of Consciousness

Past Life Therapy

In this chapter, in order to consider freedom, and especially inner freedom, I will explain the steps in the process of developing greater consciousness, as conceived by Joel L. Whitton, M.D, and by Kukai (774–835), founder of Shingon Buddhism, an esoteric sect that became one of the major schools in Japan.

Whitton has studied past life therapy for more than twenty years, and first introduced his hypnotic investigations of previous lives in his book *Life Between Life: Scientific Explorations into the Void Separating One Incarnation from the Next*. This book is based in his own experience taking patients back into past lives through hypnosis. Whitton found that the roots of people's physical or psychological problems often lay in their memories of past lives. When patients were able, in a deep trance state, to recognize the cause of their health problems, even serious diseases were occasionally healed spontaneously. Whitton became known as "the doctor of lost causes." He often writes about journeying to the world that no one has ever entered—to what he terms "the other world." In his view, human beings evolve, experiencing many interlives between death and birth. During these interlives, we recall past lives and draw up a basic plan for the next life. This concept of the cycle of birth and death as a means to increased understanding is known as "karma." We choose the milestone events that will occur in our lifetimes, so that we can learn things that we did not recognize in past lives. We may learn through suffering and bitter experience, or through constructive deeds. This probably depends on our will power and on our ability to affect our circumstances and surroundings—in other words, our creativity. Figure 21–1 diagrams Whitton's basic thought on human existence and development. He conducted clinical research into past life therapies, and concluded that human beings advance through the following five stages that may span many lifetimes.

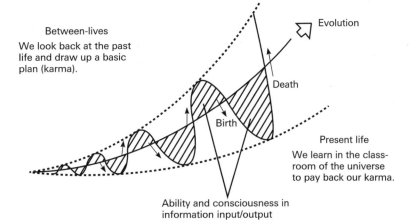

Figure 21–1
Whitton's theory of human existence and development.

1. Materialism. The search for physical well-being, a state dominated by craving and dissatisfaction. There is very little consideration for the feelings of others and philosophical goals are nonexistent. There is no recognition of an afterlife or a supreme power of any kind.

2. Superstition. The first awareness that there are forces and entities greater than oneself, although this awareness includes almost no real knowledge of this omniscient power. There is only the appreciation that something is out there that cannot be controlled, except perhaps by amulets and rituals. A materialistic lifestyle prevails here as well.

3. Fundamentalism. The practice of simple, superstitious, and rigid thinking about God or the Almighty. Such thinking becomes the rationale for living. There is a belief that prayer, adherence to ritual, and the practice of certain attitudes and behavior will guarantee the supreme reward—a place in heaven or the afterlife. A leader is usually required to intercede with the all-powerful God, who must be appeased. It matters little whether the leader is a guru who wears a turban or is called Jesus Christ; someone is needed to expound upon, harness, and direct basic conviction.

4. Philosophy. An early awakening to the awareness of responsibility for one's own actions. Religious conviction is maintained, but there is an appreciation that reliance on dogma will not suffice. This stage is marked by respect for life, tolerance of the beliefs of others, and an understanding of the deeper teachings of the orthodox religions.

5. Persecution. Characterized by inner tension and anguish that spring from an intense desire to understand the hidden

meaning of life. The awareness that existence has a profound meaning is coupled with great uncertainty as to how to apprehend that meaning. The search for answers frequently takes the form of extensive reading, study, and membership in various mystical and metaphysical groups. The title of the stage is taken from Jesus's Sermon on the Mount and the phrase "Blessed are those who are persecuted" (Matthew 5:10).

When these neophyte stages have been successfully navigated, the individual steps firmly onto a path of evolution—something like a huge mountain crossed this way and that with trails, some more heavily travelled than others. Whitton suggests that these diverse paths may lead up the Eastern side, through meditation and transcendent contemplation, or climb the Western face, through mysticism and intellectual metaphysics.

Whitton's theory is based on clinical research, and is very reliable. Although Edgar Cayce and Emanuel Swedenborg also maintained the same theories, Whitton is the only one of the three who was trained in Western medicine and who is alive today.

Wisdom of the Ancients

Kukai (pronounced "Koo-kai"), the great Japanese *qi* master, lived about twelve hundred years ago. When he was fifty-seven years old, he wrote "Treatise on the Ten Stages of the Development of Mind" in response to a command by Emperor Junna (reigned 823–833), that the heads of all the sects in the land write and submit a description of their teachings. In this work, Kukai set forth all the basic principles of esoteric Shingon teaching. Some scholars have viewed the work as a thinly veiled effort to imply that his school was superior to others. But I believe that Kukai probably only wanted to show the steps he himself had gone through to attain enlightenment, and to recommend this same process to others. When it comes to the methodology, we can consider the *san mitsu kaji*, or incantation of three secrets—that is, of body, speech and mind. The concept of "ten stages of the development of mind" is originally *himitsu mandara jujushinron* in Japanese. The word "*himitsu*" means secret. However, here it does not refer to something "hidden," but to something that cannot be described in words. The condition of being "awakened to the truth of the universe" is too subtle and too significant to express in words.

The Sanskrit term "mandala" was originally formed by adding the suffix *la* (possession or accomplishment) to the word *manda* (center, essence, true nature, or vitality). "*Manda*" means center, essence, true nature or zest, while "la" means possession or accomplishment. Thus "mandala" carries the meaning of "that which possesses the essence of basic truth." In esoteric Buddhism, *"mandara"* expresses the fullness of reaching the *"bodhi"* (awakened) state. A mandala is not just a symbolic picture; it is also reality, essence, and a process of creation. In a mandalic concept, everything is to be affirmed. Its basic essence is of cognition followed by creation. In this respect, Ken Wilber's "spectrum of consciousness" replicates the mandalic concept.

In his work, Kukai described the mind in terms of ten different levels, or stages. He suggested that proceeding through the ten stages would lead us to creative deeds—that is, would result in an evolution of consciousness. The following is my free translation of Kukai's ten stages of the development of the mind.

Kukai's stages of the development of the mind

1. Consciousness of *isho teiyo*, or, literally, "different life ram": The word *"teiyo"* means "ram." Those in this stage are concerned only with eating and with sexual and material desires. They are absolutely not interested in any philosophical considerations such as the law of cause and effect. They simply repeat death and birth throughout the cycle of their different lives.

2. Consciousness of *gudo-jisai*; "foolish child keeping morals": Those who belong to this stage have not yet come to recognized or to understand essential truths. But their Buddhanature is awakened, and they seek to purify themselves. At least they do not actively do anything bad.

3. Consciousness of *yodo-mui*; "baby no fear": Just as an infant feels safe in its mother's arms, those in this stage find peace of mind in some kind of religion or doctrine and in reliance on a leader or priest of a specific religious sect. Like a baby embraced by its mother, their viewpoint is limited.

4. Consciousness of *yui-un-muga*; "temporary body and mind, no eternal self": *"Un"* means the elements that comprise a human being. The body and mind are made with the five aggregates temporally, under internal and external conditions. These aggregates are form, sensation, perception, mental formation, and consciousness. People in the fourth stage are aware of at least one teaching of the Buddha—on the nonexistence of any immortal self.

5. Consciousness of *batsugo inju*; "taking out karma, discarding seeds of cause": In their interlives, people draw up a basic plan, including sufferings they will undergo, for the next life. This concept is known as *"go,"* or karma. *"In"* refers to causes, and those

who are in this stage begin to make an effort to get rid of karma and the twelve causes of suffering. They recognize the existence of karma and undertake practical training.

6. Consciousness of *taen daijo*; "ties to others, the Great Vehicle":
   The compassion of Mahayana Buddhism opens the way of liberation to all other people. Those who are in this stage recognize the cause of their suffering. After training to remove the cause, their power of consciousness rises; it then stays constant. These people become able to counsel others who are in trouble. When you have overcome a difficulty, don't you feel like counseling other people who are still suffering from a similar difficulty?

7. Consciousness of *kakushin fusho*; "realize basic mind, unborn":
   "*Shin*" in this word means "transcendental consciousness" —that is, basic consciousness that creates matter, events, etc. Once consciousness is recognized, *fusho* (a state of being "unborn") will occur, making the seventh stage in this sense "opposite" the first stage; those who have reached this stage are no longer within the cycle of reincarnation. They entrust themselves completely to the large current of evolution. To express this metaphorically, a set of wooden clogs and a statue of the Buddha can both be carved from the same piece of wood. These forms may seem quite different, but in fact the difference is illusory, since the material is the same. People at this level are aware that the difference is illusory, and that clogs are at least as important as statues of the Buddha.

8. Consciousness of *ichido-mui*; "universal justice, no artifice":
   Kukai used the word "secret" for this stage, because it is difficult to describe it in words. Once you apprehend the laws of nature and of the universe you suddenly become one and at peace with the universe.

9. Consciousness of *gokumu jisho*; "extreme nothing self nature":
   Originally, "*mu*" means "no existence," but here it means an inexhaustible base that brings forth everything. Restated in a more casual way, it can be said to mean "a field of unity." Having reached the field of unity, one's consciousness becomes himself. In this stage, like the holy man Saibaba in India, materialization from empty space seems possible.

10. Consciousness of *himitsu sogon*; "secret sublime":
    "*Himitsu*" is "secret," which simply means here that it cannot be expressed in words. "*Sogon*" refers to that state in which things that are good or evil, right or bad, beautiful or ugly, and past or future are all affirmed and glittering with solemnity.

Death the Road to Rebirth

Consciousness seems to progress stage by stage, probably at first switching back and forth—going forward and then back among two or three consecutive stages. For instance, while those who oscillate between the first and second stages will gradually advance to be born in the third stage, once they have reached the fourth or fifth stage, they will no longer return to the first.

By now, you are aware of the consensus between the theories put forth by Kukai and Joel L. Whitton. When I first discovered that the content of the first and the fifth stage were exactly the same, I was stunned, yet I intuited that this might be true. I studied the theories of Ken Wilber, Joel L. Whitton, and Kukai, in an effort to completely reconsider the concept of inner freedom. After all, if you are aware that everything is evolving, you will view things positively, in keeping with the mandalic concept, despite various undesirable conditions or difficulties in your life. In fact, it is possible to see the stages of consciousness very clearly when we use Kukai's "Ten Stages of the Development of Mind" that sharply illuminates and distinguishes the various levels of consciousness. But we must avoid ranking or criticizing others, since taking this kind of attitude would run contrary to the concept that characterizes the tenth stage, "Everything is to be affirmed." Anyway, I would suggest that Kukai, Wilber, and Whitton—great teachers of religion, psychology, and medicine from the past and present— have set up guideposts to show us where we are, to enable us to proceed more quickly and more comfortably.

Yukio Funai of the Funai Institute in Tokyo has written on the concept of "this world and the other world": "Our home seems to be in the other world. Our true form is a soul, i.e., a form of consciousness. If no provision were made for this, we might miss our real home, when we come to the boarding school called Earth. So all memory of our real home is temporarily erased when we are born. Our body has its limitations, which make it necessary for us study. If we do not put forth a great deal of effort, life will be quite tough on us. We are trapped in the body, which is a fairly inconvenient vessel. In the other world, we were able to see everything. We could know with certainty how others felt, and we could exist anywhere, immediately, as we wished. But, when life grew too easy and comfortable there, we tended to become lazy. That's why souls were sent to this world, where everyone must live by their own efforts. That way, ambition and a competitive spirit can be encouraged. While we learn, our vessel (body) gets old sooner or later and breaks down. Then we can finally go back to our real home. In order to learn efficiently, souls who knew each other well in the other world are often transferred to this world in a group. Every record in this school is saved because it will serve as reference for choosing the next school, time frame, vessel, or companions. Anything the soul learns in one life will again be its property in the other world, and will also be 'transferred' to the next life. You can probably imagine well enough how the law of causation works. It might be in order, if human beings don't know about the other world or are not aware that death is not the end. I think that humans' level of consciousness has evolved, so that we gradually understand more about the principles of life and death. Human beings are slowly moving closer to God, and not to beasts. That's why we should make efforts to know more about the law of nature."

XXII — The Three Mysteries

Develop Your Own Paranormal Abilities

Since ancient times and in every part of the world, people with paranormal abilities far beyond the bounds of the ordinary have appeared, and today their teachings can be found everywhere. But what practitioners and martial artists need to know are not teachings so much as practical methods and techniques. In formulating my method, I have attached great weight to practical, rather than strictly philosophical or religious, concerns. In doing so, I have brought to bear my years of experience as a doctor and as a martial artist. I extracted the elements that I consider most important and effective from many different teachings, methods, books, and experiments. In this way my own style of *qigong* evolved gradually, while incorporating many influences.

All of my studies and experiments have led me finally to conclude that Kukai is the greatest teacher who ever lived. In 804 Kukai—who would later return to Japan to establish an esoteric school of Japanese Buddhism—went to China as a student monk to study with the Chinese patriarch. He had, however, already mastered most of the esoteric tradition before even leaving for China. In his *Sokushin jobutsu-gi* ("Attaining Enlightenment in This Present Body," included in *Major Works*), Kukai wrote about the differences between exoteric and esoteric Buddhism, and about how to unite with the Dharmakaya Buddha and attain enlightenment. Esoteric Buddhism and the teachings of Kukai are rather difficult to understand, but they also have an extremely clear and practical aspect which will be my focus here. For several years, I have been working on how best to express Kukai's philosophy and method, trying to incorporate these into my system of *qigong* exercise and make them more easily accesible.

I would like to introduce here a few basic points of esoteric Buddhism. In *Sokushin jobutsu-gi*, Kukai writes, "When the Grace of the Three

Mysteries is retained, our inborn three mysteries will quickly be manifested." Of the various Buddhist schools, only esoteric Shingon Buddhism teaches that it is possible to attain enlightenment "in this very body" (*sokushin jobutsu*). All other Buddhist traditions teach that one must wait for rebirth into another world in order to attain enlightenment.

The "three mysteries" refers to the transformation of the physical, verbal, and mental activities of human beings into more highly developed stages—that is, into mysteries of the body, mysteries of speech, and mysteries of the mind. Mysteries of the body include forming mudras with the hands, while mysteries of speech include the chanting of mantras, and mysteries of the mind include visualizing the Buddha. In other words, the hands play a significant role in the mysteries of the body, while language is central to mysteries of speech, and mysteries of mind refers largely to image-building.

When we consider these mysteries in the context of the functioning of the brain, the "body" can be seen as including the motor center; "speech," the sense of hearing and the speech-control center; and "mind," the sense of sight and the ability to visualize. Grace works to augment brain functioning, and makes it possible, when the practitioner concentrates the mind on a single point, to gather and retain energy from the universe. Interestingly enough, there is a legend which holds that Kukai demonstrated these truths by changing his body to golden light, in the presence of the emperor and a group of monks from other Buddhist schools. I personally think that this story is true, because after this incident, Buddhist monks of other schools stopped arguing against Kukai's teaching that one can attain enlightenment here and now, in the temporal body. Also, when we release or receive extremely high-level *qi* energy, golden light is sometimes actually visible.

The Three Mysteries as Qi Training

When we analyze the Grace of the Three Mysteries from the perspective of brain physiology, its powerful function is clear and reasonable. The brain can eliminate worldly thoughts when we simultaneously activate the motor center, of our fingers, the auditory and speech centers, the visual input center, and the ability to visualize clearly. At this stage the voluntary parts of the brain are almost completely occupied, and there is no room for worldly thoughts to enter. I think that the Grace of the Three Mysteries is the best method for the development of our abilities. No other method can surpass it as long as human beings exist in their present form, with both a body and a brain.

Our physical activity, verbal activity, and mental activity are all transformed to the higher level of the three mysteries (Figure 22–1). Esoteric monks practice various methods, such as making a holy fire for invocation, to change the three actions into three mysteries. However, such training is not available to ordinary people. That is why I arranged the Grace of the Three Mysteries for use in *qigong* (Figure 22–2). If you practice *qigong*, you can understand the meaning of releasing *qi* from your hands or using your hands as a sensor. In fact, the training of making a *qi* ball between the palms is a form of training in the mystery of the body. When you release *qi* from both hands and at the same time sense *qi*, you are creating feedback circuits of "input" and "output," which enable you immediately to sense the effect of what you have done. Using this method, the brain develops very quickly and your ability can grow accordingly.

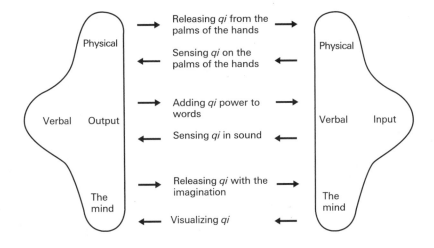

Figure 22–1
Input-output feedback circuit of the Grace of the Three Mysteries.

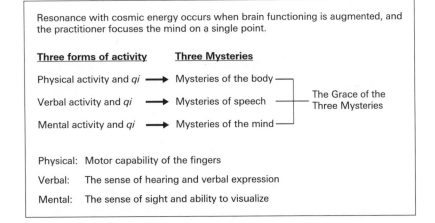

Figure 22–2
The Grace of the Three Mysteries and *qi*.

Kukai's Experience

When Kukai was twenty-four years old, he wrote of his experience in his first work *Sango-shiiki* (Indications of the Goals of the Three Teachings), in which he described the energy of sound and *qi*, and that of vision and *qi*. Let me quote from his description: "At eighteen I entered the college in the capital and studied diligently. Meanwhile a Buddhist monk showed me a scripture called *Kokuzo gumonji no ho*. It stated that if one recites the mantra one million times according to the proper method, one will be able to memorize passages and understand the meaning of any scripture. Believing what Buddha says to be true, I recited the mantra incessantly, as if I were rubbing one piece of wood against another to make fire, all the while earnestly hoping to achieve this result. I climbed up Mount Dairyo in Awa province and meditated at Cape Muroto in Tosa. The valley reverberated to the sound of my voice as I recited, and the planet Venus appeared in the sky."

This ascetic method, called "*kokuzo gumonji no ho*," is still practiced even today in esoteric Buddhism. "*Kokuzo*" means "sky." If a person masters this method, he should be able to memorize sounds he has heard—even if they are as limitless as the limitless sky. Kukai was already known as a genius even in childhood, but when he mastered this method he came to be called the "greatest genius." Though this practice is effective, it is obviously not for everyone. For that very reason, I became enthusiastic about the possibility of finding a new method to replace the ascetic way, so that those not as gifted as Kukai could undergo similar experiences. I focused on the technique of the Grace of the Three Mysteries, and was again struck by its practical excellence—that is, the great effect it has of concentrating the three main functions of the brain—stimulation from the fingers; listening and talking; and visualization—into a single focal point.

The sentence, "The valley reverberated to the sound of my voice as I recited and the planet Venus appeared in the sky" contains a very deep meaning. The reverberations of the mantra that Kukai recited turned his whole existence toward the reverberation of the sound. And then, the valley—in other words, the natural world around him—began to vibrate with his mantra. Thus he experienced oneness with the universe. He saw a light reminiscent of Venus behind his closed eyes. He expressed the fullness of his gratitude to the life energy seen everywhere in nature. Such moments of oneness and gratitude are the moments at which the brain can expand the range of its total understanding until it is as broad and limitless as the sky. This is far beyond any question of ego. The secret of the method which made Kukai an unparalleled genius was in providing stimulation to the brain with sound and in an image-building power that was so strong that Kukai could "see" Venus with his eyes closed.

Mystic Verse: The Mantra

Since the brain is protected by the thick cranium, the only way to stimulate it directly is through sound. But just how can this be done? Kukai recited the mantra wholeheartedly in a cave. The cave would then have provided a high level of reverberation. The humming sound caused by this reverberation would have streamed into Kukai's brain. So, for the Grace of the Three Mysteries, you must visualize an object that is beyond yourself and keep sending sound from the oral cavity to the deep center of the brain.

When you add the sense of *qi* to the sense of sight, touch, and hearing, you emerge with a magnified sensibility. Then you can bring the input system of information, which flows into the brain, to its highest level. Through this process you can improve your ability to perceive and understand.

How about *qi* borne along on sound? How do we cause *qi* energy to be borne by an image? Think of the singers, musicians, or even the public speakers who move our hearts. Don't we feel their *qi* energy borne along on their voices or their instruments? In the martial arts, "yelling" is a central part of the action. In the Rinzai school of Zen, monks "roar." These are all examples of the way *qi* energy can be borne on the voice. To bear *qi* energy in an image is the highest level of *qi* technique. Most people think that vision is only intended for input of information (by actual, physical seeing), but if you can visualize an image vividly with your eyes closed, you will be able to use your vision to create something, in a process analogous to making something out of clay with your hands.

OM Qigong

Esoteric Buddhism is a complete and essential system of human evolution, and the Grace of the Three Mysteries is an effective method for focusing and sharpening brain functioning. The more you realize how powerful is the effect of the Grace of the Three Mysteries, the more you begin to want to learn and master the technique. It is possible to train independently, using techniques from esoteric Buddhism such as mudras, mantras, and meditation on the Buddha. But I was reluctant to try to introduce OM *qigong* as a *qigong* method. I once taught some *qi* friends certain esoteric mantras. The whole experience fell rather flat, as they weren't particulary interested in learning mantras, and I wasn't so keen on teaching them either. This only confirmed my suspicion that training with a religious orientation would not be easily accepted by people in the modern world. Modern people, I thought, would want something they could understand with their reason, not just with their spirit. I wanted to find a different training method, suited to this culture and this age. At first I thought I would try the Chinese method "Liu-Zi-Que" ("Six-letter method") a *qigong* practice which involves uttering six Chinese characters. I did find a teacher who had been trained in this method in China. But the letters need to be pronounced in Chinese, which I thought could be a stumbling-block to non-native Chinese speakers. After a good deal of searching, I discovered the Tenshin-goso of Shintaido. When I had been studying Karate quite a few years ago, a friend who was then practicing Shintaido taught me some of that tradition's mysteries. Today I realize how beneficial this discipline is as *qi* training, but I was not aware of its effects at that time, and after a while stopped practicing the things he taught me. Then, several years ago, I met Hiroyuki Aoki, the founder of Shintaido. In the Tenshin-goso exercise, which he originally created on the basis of his experience in the martial arts, one utters the five vowels, *a-e-i-o-u* (pronounced *ah, eh, ii, oh, oo*), bringing both hands straight down with each utterance in a "Karate blow" that strikes the air.

By combining the Tenshin-goso with Kukai's method, I developed what I call "OM *qigong*." This adaptation of the ancient method now means that anyone can practice the Grace of Three Mysteries without needing to overcome psychological resistance.

Experience It Yourself

When you utter "OM," the vowel sound resonates in the head, stimulating the brain. This is a method of concentrating the mind. Kukai discusses the mystery of speech in his *Shoji jisso-gi* ("The Meanings of Sound, Word and Reality"). His thoughts can be summarized in this way: All things revealed in the universe have sound—that is, vibration. The vibration of a mantra is deep, universal, and basic. By reciting a mantra, you can resonate in synch with other existences and can can come to know the true nature of all things, or reality.

In esoteric Buddhism, seven vocal organs are mentioned; the top of the head, the gums, the teeth, the lips, tongue, the throat, and the chest. In OM *qigong*, when the brain is directly stimulated by the sounds *a-e-i-o-u*, each Chakra in the body corresponds to a particular sound. While "looking" at the Chakras with our mind's eye, stimulate them with a *qi* ball that you make between your palms (Figure 22–3). Stimulating Chakras with the *qi* ball corresponds to creating the "esoteric body." Sending the vowel sounds *a-e-i-o-u* into each Chakra is an element of "esoteric speech," while visualizing *qi* of earth and space flowing into each Chakra is part of the "esoteric mind."

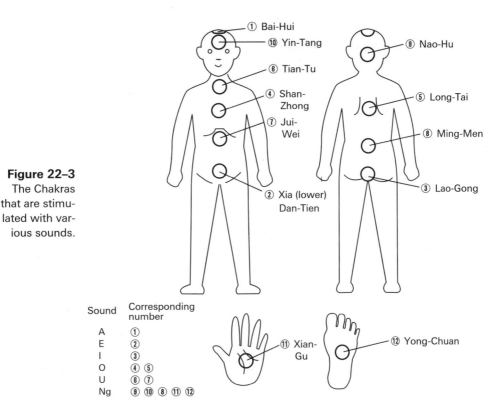

Figure 22–3
The Chakras that are stimulated with various sounds.

① Bai-Hui
⑩ Yin-Tang
⑥ Tian-Tu
④ Shan-Zhong
⑦ Jui-Wei
② Xia (lower) Dan-Tien
⑨ Nao-Hu
⑤ Long-Tai
⑧ Ming-Men
③ Lao-Gong

Sound	Corresponding number
A	①
E	②
I	③
O	④ ⑤
U	⑥ ⑦
Ng	⑨ ⑩ ⑧ ⑪ ⑫

⑪ Xian-Gu
⑫ Yong-Chuan

I recorded the vowel sound with a heightened resonance that mimicked the experience of being in a cave. Listening to the tape through stereo headphones, repeat the sounds that you hear on the tape. Let your voice resonate with the sound of the tape in the head. When the sound resonates in a humming fashion, you will feel comfortable, as if your brain were under a pleasant shower. Sooner or later, you will understand Kukai's description, "The valley reverberated to the sound of my voice as I recited." When you reach this stage, you will be able to see colors with your eyes closed. The color will change with the Chakra being stimulated. Take it easy and enjoy the beauty of the colors. If you want to practice without the tape, the bath may be a good place. Relax in the bathtub and utter "A-E-I-O-U."

The Whole Body as Chakra

OM *qigong* can also be used for the Microcosmic or Macrocosmic Orbit methods. To use OM *qigong* with the Microcosmic Orbit method, absorb *qi* from the top of the head (Bai-Hui) and circulate it along Ren-Mai and Du-Mai while uttering "*a*" (pronounced *ah*). The direction in which to circulate it will depend on whether your *qi* flows in the male or female direction. Then say the rest of the vowels in the same way. To use it with the Macrocosmic Orbit method, absorb *qi* from Bai-Hui, allowing every cell in your body to vibrate, and expand the *qi* vibration together with the sound. If you continue, your entire body will eventually come to function as one Chakra. This is the stage of the Transcendental Orbit. At this stage, no one and nothing can even influence your *qi* field any more, let alone disturb it. In Peking when I met Master Zhao Guang I had a strong sense that he had reached this level. The method of OM *qigong* that I have developed offers you an opportunity to know the Transcendental Orbit. Try placing a vajra on different parts of your body, and you will be able to sense if *qi* diminishes. If you are at the level of the Transcendental Orbit, your *qi* cannot be affected by a vajra.

By the way, there is another method for concentrating the mystery of speech and the mystery of the mind in the hypothalamus and the pituitary gland, but this method may be a little dangerous, because untrained practitioners could upset the balance of the autonomic nervous system. I do not recommend this method for everyone, but only to people who have mastered the Macrocosmic Orbit method with OM *qigong*. However, this method does make possible the stimulation of the A-10 nerve that was discussed in Chapter XV. With it, you can achieve nearly the same effect as you would from the Grace of the Three Mysteries, simply by repeating the basic OM *qigong*.

Try the following test: After practicing OM *qigong* for ten or fifteen minutes, draw a circle on your arm with a ballpoint pen. Then make a *qi* ball between your palms and imagine that pure blood and *qi* energy are flowing into the circle you just drew. Say to yourself that the cells within this area will be able to bear any kind of stimulation. Then pinch the circled area. You should not feel pain, no matter how hard you squeeze. Or you may feel a bit of pain at first, but you will probably notice, if you try pinching other parts of your arm, that the pain you feel inside the circle is much less inside than outside.

This test serves as evidence that we can change our sensory perceptions by controlling the brain. You have probably heard of Yoga ascetics piercing their flesh with needles, or walking over burning coals. I believe that they do this by learning to deliberately release endorphins—neurotransmitters that act as a "natural morphine," regulating pain and producing pleasure—into the brain. During experiments of this sort, I began to realize that the conscious body is not identical with the brain, but uses the brain to communicate with the physical world.

They say that the A-10 nerve controls pleasant sensations such as sexual desire, appetite, creativity, and even enlightenment. I think that one purpose of training in esoteric Buddhism is to convert pleasant sensations directly connected with survival into pleasant sensations of creativity or enlightenment, through the Grace of Three Mysteries. This would explain why desire is affirmed in esoteric Buddhism.

The Heart Sutra of Kukai

Master Zhao Guang has said, "The origin of *qi* is Nothingness. Nothingness is the only origin of reality that cannot be proven. In Buddhism, it is called Emptiness."

I have always been concerned with finding practical methods and techniques. Since I am a long-time practitioner of *qi*, armchair philosophy on Nothingness or Emptiness has never satisfied me. In my research, I have investigated techniques, trying to find a level at which technique would give way to something more. And yet I also did want to understand the true meaning of Nothingness, or Emptiness. At first I was not sure if I understood it correctly. Now that I have reached the level of the Macrocosmic Orbit and have trained in OM *qigong*, which is a modern adaptation of the Grace of the Three Mysteries, I think I can explain Nothingness.

If you are involved in Buddhism or Yoga, you may have heard of the *Hannya shingyo*, or Heart Sutra, an exoteric Buddhist scripture written in Sanskrit on the topic of Emptiness; it remains today one of the most popular Buddhist scriptures in Japan. Kukai interpreted this work from an esoteric point of view in his commentary *Hannya shingyo hiken* ("The Secret Key to the Heart Sutra" (included in *Major Works*). Kukai divides the sutra into five parts, and it is the *way* he divided them that proves his genius. The following are a few quotes.

"When the Bodhisattva Avalokitesvara was practicing profound Transcendental Wisdom, he discerned clearly that Five Psychophysical Constituents are empty and thereby became free from all sufferings." (Part 1)

"O Sariputra, form is emptiness, emptiness is form; form is no other than emptiness, emptiness is no other than form. Of sensation, conception, predisposition, and consciousness the same can be said. O Sariputra, all things are characterized by emptiness; they are neither born nor do they perish; they are neither tainted nor immaculate; neither do they increase nor decrease. Therefore, in emptiness there is no form, no sensation, no conception, no predisposition, no consciousness; no eyes, ear, nose, tongue, body, mind; no form, sound, scent, physical sensation, objects of mind; no realm of vision ... no realm of consciousness. There is no ignorance ... no old age and death, no extinction of old age and death. There is no suffering, no accumula-

tion, no annihilation, no Noble Paths. There is no wisdom and no attainment because there is no object to be attained."
(Part 2)

"The bodhisattva has no obstacle in mind because of his dependence on Transcendental Wisdom; because he has no obstacles, he has no fear. Being free from all perverted views, he reaches ultimate Nirvana. All the Buddha of the past, present, and future, depending on Transcendental Wisdom, attain perfect enlightenment."
(Part 3)

"Therefore, one knows that the Prajna-paramita is the great mantra, the mantra of great wisdom, the highest mantra, the peerless mantra, which is capable of allaying all suffering; it is true and not false."
(Part 4)

"Gate gate paragate parasamgate bodhi svaha."
(Part 5)

Notes

Bodhisattva Avalokiesvara: A person who engages in the practice.
The Five Psychological Constituents: Form, sensation, conception, volition, and consciousness.
Sariputra: Proper name; a character to whom the Buddha speaks.
Nirvana: The goal of spiritual practice.
(Part 5, it should be noted, is the mystic mantra. It is chanted in Sanskrit because each word contains mystic power.)

The sutra can be briefly outlined as follows. In Part 1, a practitioner is training in an effort to learn to recognize the visible and invisible worlds, and comprehends that the five factors—form, sensation, conception, volition, and consciousness—constituting the self and all other existences are Emptiness. With this, he is freed from all suffering and misfortune. Part 2 discusses the nature of Emptiness. Part 3 outlines the way to Emptiness and the benefits to be derived from it. Parts 4 and 5 introduce the mystic formula for chanting.

Study alone does not bring real knowledge of Emptiness; this knowledge only comes with experience.

In Buddhism, the six curricula, known as the Six Paramitas, are introduced as steps in the training for people who seek profound wisdom. In modern terms, the Six Paramitas can be expressed as charity, morality, patience, effort, meditation, and wisdom.

The Six Paramitas

1. Charity Paramita: Give to others what you have, including material objects, time, money, and even *qi* energy. Share your knowledge with others and teach techniques. Diminish your ego.
2. Morality Paramita: Cultivate a habit of living in accordance with your conscience. Reduce the likelihood of your having cause for regret.
3. Patience Paramita: Accept others and the things that happen to us. Diminish anger.
4. Effort Paramita: Realize that everything is in the process of evolution. Do not relax your efforts.
5. Meditation Paramita: Open the window of your mind. Awaken more of the hidden capacity of your brain, which will enable you to recognize the truth of the physical world.
6. Wisdom Paramita: Train in the Six Paramitas and increase your wisdom.

If you wish to better understand the Six Paramitas, thinking of the opposite behavior will help. If your ego comes out, you will lose your sense of right judgment. If you do something that goes against your conscience, you will feel badly. If you get angry with someone, it will be hard to keep calm and you will not be able to meditate. The first four Paramitas are exoteric; the fifth contains an element of esotericism—that is, practical training for body and mind. You can practice the first through fourth Paramitas each day until they become an integral part of your life. Keep your mind open and relaxed, so that harmful "data" does not have a chance to accumulate. However, all of this by itself will still not bring you knowledge of Emptiness.

The Technique for Reaching Emptiness

According to Kukai's "*Hannya shigyo hiken*," training to gain wisdom leads to the gate for *samadhi*. The word *samadhi* is actually central to my method of *qigong* training, because it is key to understanding Emptiness. What is *samadhi*?

The Yoga Sutra speaks of "eight limbs." These are restraint, observation, postures, regulation of the breath, drawing the senses inward for calming the mind, concentration, meditation, and superconsciousness. The last three are the *sammaya* ("inner limbs"). The *sammaya* is a series of spiritual exercises, the last stage of which is superconsciousness, or *samadhi*. As Swami Vishnu explains in *The Sivananda Companion to Yoga*, "During concentration, one keeps a tight rein on the mind;

during meditation, the rein is no longer necessary, for the mind stays on its own accord on one single thought wave. The eighth [limb] is *samadhi*, or superconsciousness, a state beyond time, space, and causation where body and mind are transcended and total unity exists. In *samadhi*, the meditator and the object of concentration become one."

The Grace of the Three Mysteries is the concrete method of psychological techniques or usage of the brain. Through the Grace of the Three Mysteries you must focus the brain on one concentration point, and you will reach the stage where you become one with the object of your concentration.

The Last Step

Now, you need to take one more step to reach Emptiness. While meditating, abruptly cut off the connection between your target of concentration and your consciousness of self. You will probably feel as if your mind is empty, as if you are thinking of nothing at all despite your clarity of mind, as if you were suddenly able to perceive all the existences everywhere at the same time, or as if you exist everywhere although you do recognize the specific place where you are. You will feel oneness between the target and your consciousness. At this stage, try visualizing something, using your firm belief. There is a good chance that the object you visualize will actually materialize.

Let me introduce one of the practical methods for reaching Emptiness. Bring OM *qigong* as the Grace of the Three Mysteries into imagination. This is the so-called Grace of the One Mystery. Then suddenly stop doing OM *qigong*. You will feel as if you are surrounded by the sound of stillness, or as if you are alone in a mountain forest. While in this stage, visualize a painful part of the body and think of it as being healed. When you visualize this part of the body as healed, the pain will disappear. I tried this method with a patient who had gout and was unable to walk. When I was in the stage of Emptiness, I visualized the painful part of his body as being completely well. His pain disappeared completely. I believe I may have been more surprised than he was.

I have recently been recommending this exercise to my *qi* colleagues as a means of reaching Emptiness, and it has been very successful. But it is also important to keep to a routine of basic physical training in the Microcosmic Orbit method. You must also be able to inhale *qi* from space through the Macrocosmic Orbit method, and must follow the Six Paramitas to keep the mind clear and calm. The stage of *samadhi* is marked by regular, constant brain wave patterns. For instance, laser beams with even wave lengths are able to penetrate an iron board, although white light with uneven wave lengths is not able to (Figure 22–4). In the same way, regular brain waves lead to improved brain functioning, and help us to use our conscious energy to affect the outside world. Some of the information in this chapter may be a bit difficult, but I believe that it will be of use particularly to people who have already spent some time searching for a "way" with which they can be comfortable.

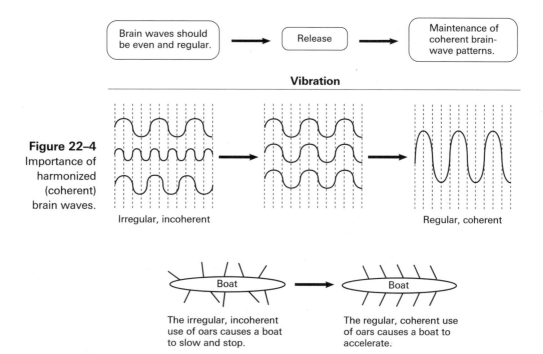

Figure 22–4 Importance of harmonized (coherent) brain waves.

XXIII — Samadhi to Emptiness

The Finger-Counting Method

Your ability to visualize will surely improve with this next exercise, the secret of which lies in your fingers. Known as the finger-counting method, it is one of the techniques of the Grace of the Three Mysteries—more specifically, the first step (Figure 23–1). Toyoji Komura, a specialist in Japanese religion and Buddhism and an expert on pendulums, taught me a method for rapidly improving the ability to concentrate, which I then rearranged for my *qigong* method. This will not only improve the dexterity of your hands, but also help you improve your visualization ability.

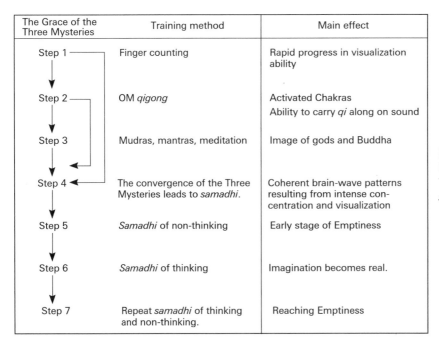

The Grace of the Three Mysteries	Training method	Main effect
Step 1	Finger counting	Rapid progress in visualization ability
Step 2	OM *qigong*	Activated Chakras Ability to carry *qi* along on sound
Step 3	Mudras, mantras, meditation	Image of gods and Buddha
Step 4	The convergence of the Three Mysteries leads to *samadhi*.	Coherent brain-wave patterns resulting from intense concentration and visualization
Step 5	*Samadhi* of non-thinking	Early stage of Emptiness
Step 6	*Samadhi* of thinking	Imagination becomes real.
Step 7	Repeat *samadhi* of thinking and non-thinking.	Reaching Emptiness

Figure 23–1
From the Grace of the Three Mysteries to *samadhi*.

If we stare at an object and then shut our eyes, it is difficult to visualize the object. The image disappears after just a second, because we have no mechanism to retain it as an image. But when we look at our fingers, the situation is different. The brain recognizes the movement and conditions of the fingers in the motor center and sensory center almost perfectly. This helps us to set about building an image through our visual center, and to build a "three-dimensional television" in the brain. Continually practicing this method while visualizing the fingers will soon make it possible to "see" other images in this "television" as well, and eventually to control them.

In this exercise (see below), you will simply repeat the process of counting on your fingers between one and ten, forward and backward, while curling the fingers down toward the palm and then straightening them, one by one. After repeating this sequence ten times, go on to step 4 of the Grace of the Three Mysteries (see Figure 23–1). In step 4, no actual movement or speech is necessary, but you should visualize the finger counting. This training is done to gather the energy of the Three Mysteries, which makes the brain function more clearly and coherently.

After a while, you will notice that this exercise takes a lot more energy than you initially thought. In fact, step 4 will be very difficult if you have not yet mastered the Microcosmic Orbit method. And you must also be able to absorb *qi* from earth and space with the Macrocosmic Orbit method. Step 2 in Figure 23–1 is OM *qigong*, while step 3 includes mudras, mantras and meditation. You can also try step 4 after steps 1 or 2, omitting step 3, if you want to avoid religious elements from esoteric Buddhism altogether.

You must maintain the vision on the three-dimensional "television screen" of your brain as you visualize the finger counting ten times. The best time to perform the finger-counting training is right after you finish the Microcosmic and Macrocosmic Orbit methods, because it becomes easier to concentrate as your *qi* power accumulates.

Try step 3, too, if you are interested. By learning to visualize a world beyond the self, you will come to understand the significance of the visualization of gods or the Buddha. You will come to know the true meaning of the grace of which Kukai spoke. Grace is known as "*kaji*" in Japanese. According to Kukai, "*ka*" refers to the basic energy of the universe flowing into a person, while "*ji*" suggests that the person receives and holds onto that energy.

The finger-counting exercise

1. Place your palms together, then move the fingers of one hand just slightly between the fingers of the other hand (Figure 23–2).

2. Apply pressure as you rub the fingers of both hands together. The fingers must be rubbed thoroughly until they become warm, especially the sides of the fingers, from base to fingertip.

3. Move your right palm to the back of your left hand, again interlacing the fingertips, and rub. Rub the sides of the fingers well, too. (Note: Take particular care to rub the sides of the little fingers and the thumbs, because they tend to move away from the hand.)

4. Move your left palm to the back of your right hand and rub again. Rub the sides of fingers well.

5. Bring your palms toward your face, and notice the sensation of heat given off by your palms. This is caused by the higher temperature that accompanies improved circulation of blood through the hands. Imagine that there is an invisible *qi* ball the size of a softball between your palms, and you will likely sense heat in the air, or a feeling of repulsion or tingling.

6. Open your hands and hold them about thirty centimeters from your face.

7. Bend the fingers down toward your palm slowly, one at a time, starting with the thumb of your right hand, and at the same time count backward from ten in a language in which you are not fluent. (If you are learning Spanish, count in Spanish. If you are taking a course in Russian, count in that language.) It is necessary to count in a language that is not your mother tongue, because this will help you to concentrate, and intense concentration as you count is necessary for brain functioning during this exercise. While you count, stare at your fingers as they move.

8. When you finish counting and bending the fingers downward one by one, begin opening the fingers one by one, beginning with the left thumb, counting upward from one. Repeat steps 7 and 8 until you have done both about ten times.

9. Now stare at each finger carefully as you count and then, after counting one finger, close your eyes and try to visualize the movement that you just saw. "Print" the movement on the "screen" in your eyes, as if you were taking a picture of the finger with a camera. Repeat this step several times.

10. In this step, shut your eyes and again do the process of moving and counting the fingers, as above. Throughout, visualize the movement of fingers vividly. Repeat.

11. Again, your eyes should be shut, but this time do not move the fingers at all. Count the fingers slowly by means of visualization only.

12. Make a *qi* ball between your palms and again visualize the movement of your fingers. The *qi* ball will be strengthened.

13. Visualize the movement of fingers and also the counting, but without any physical movement. Continue until the image is so vivid that you can "see" it with your eyes closed.

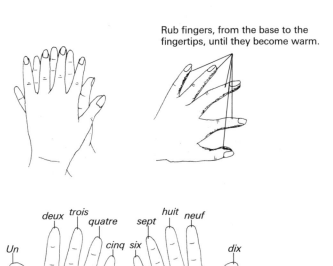

Figure 23–2
The finger-counting exercise.

Non-Thinking and Consciousness

Now we are standing at the entry to Emptiness. I am calling step 5 "the *samadhi* of non-thinking." If you can visualize finger-counting for ten rounds, step 5 will be easy. After practicing step 4 in the three-dimensional television of the brain, all you have to do is abruptly switch the "television screen" off. This may be easier if you inhale once deeply and then exhale very deeply (in the Raku-raku breathing method described in Chapter III), with your shoulders relaxed and buttocks slightly tightened. In this stage, although the brain is functioning coherently, you should not be thinking of anything. You may feel as if the inside of your brain is blank. Descriptions of this stage differ from one person to the next. After you complete this stage, perform step 4 again and you should be able to enter deeper *samadhi* (Figure 23–3), but this time you are conscious. Then, turn off the "television" again for even deeper *samadhi* of non-thinking. Step 7 is to repeat *samadhi* under conditions of consciousness and non-thinking.

If you visualize something—a goal for instance—clearly while in the *samadhi* of non-thinking, the object that you visualize will become reality. If you enter ever-deeper *samadhi* of non-thinking, you will be in the world of Emptiness.

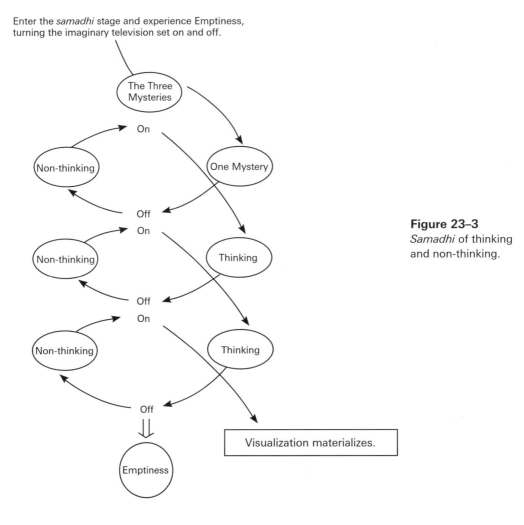

Figure 23–3
Samadhi of thinking and non-thinking.

This method is unique. You won't find it anywhere else, even in Xian-Dao, the martial arts, the medical arts, or Yoga. It is a technique for making the brain fully functional and coherent. Nowadays, various methods of meditation and training in visualization are popular, but none is more effective or powerful than the method which Kukai devised more than a thousand years ago. The more you learn this technique, the more you will realize how excellent it is. It is no exaggeration to say that the physical exercises of *qigong* exist in order to build the foundation that brings the Grace of the Three Mysteries into effect. As long as we human beings have a brain and a physical body, I can assure you that there will be no other method that can rival training in the Grace of the Three Mysteries, in terms of the higher level of consciousness which it makes possible. Someday someone may invent a method that is superior to Kukai's technique, but the only margin for such improvement that I can imagine is if the human sense of eyesight, sense of hearing, and sensation could all be developed and magnified by means of, for instance, computerization.

Actually various technologies that stimulate the brain by directing light or sound to it, including the "brain machine" and virtual reality, are available today. Yet none of these rivals Kukai's techniques. Even now, more more than a thousand years after Kukai lived, no system has been developed that would equal the effectiveness of the basic concept of the Three Mysteries and the grace with which we visualize a supreme target.

XXIV — The Gate to the Light

Lao-Tzu and Nothingness

As we near the end of our discussion of *qigong*, it seems appropriate to return to Lao-Tzu. While Confucius discussed mainly rules governing people's behavior in society, Lao-Tzu threw light upon the laws of the universe and the nature of all living creatures. The concept of Tao has always fascinated people.

"Tao gave birth to the One; the One gave birth successively to two things, three things, up to ten thousand. These ten thousand creatures cannot turn their backs to the shade without having the sun on their bellies, and it is on this blending of the breaths that their harmony depends."
(Chapter XLII)

"For though all creatures under heaven are the products of Being,
Being itself is the product of Not-being."
(Chapter XL)

The opening line of *Tao Te Ching*, "Tao gave birth to the One," can be interpreted as meaning, "Tao gave birth to the One Tao from Nothingess." Tao creates all things and Tao is the prime mover. Nothingness (Not-being) does not mean empty space, but an inexhaustible capacity. The creative action of Tao is brought forth as the admixture and mutual action of Yin *qi* and Yang *qi*; it gives birth to vital power harmonized with Yin and Yang.

"There was something formless yet complete,
That existed before heaven and earth;
Without sound, without substance,
Dependent on nothing, unchanging,

All pervading, unfailing.
One may think of it as the mother of all things under heaven.
Its true name we do not know;
'Way' is the by-name that we give it.
Were I forced to say to what class of things it belongs I should call it
　　Great (*ta*)."
(Chapter XXV)

When you read these chapters using your visualization ability, you may have a vision of primal chaos beginning to evolve slowly, like particles in primordial soup, producing various things little by little. Interestingly enough, the Tai-ji diagram looks very much like a spiralling cluster of stars (Figures 24–1 and 24–2).

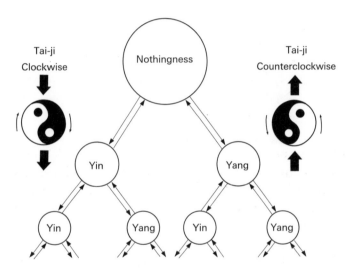

Figure 24–1
Yin and Yang in constant transformation.

In the Yang philosophy we divide things into two and then integrate them once again. The clockwise Tai-ji diagram symbolizes the creation of all things when Nothingness is transformed into Yin and Yang. The counterclockwise Tai-ji diagram symbolizes the opposite process (Yin and Yang unite and return to Nothingness). We can think of this as a never-ending process of differentiation and union, development and decline, birth and death. But we should note that while Yin and Yang are each constantly evolving and disappearing, each also contains the other.

"The Way that can be told of is not an Unvarying Way;
The names that can be named are not unvarying names.
It was from the Nameless that Heaven and Earth sprang;
The named is but the mother that rears the ten thousand creatures,
　　each after its kind.
Truly, 'Only he that rids himself forever of desire can see the Secret
　　Essences';
He that has never rid himself of desire can see only the Outcomes.

These two things issued from the same mould, but nevertheless are
   different in name.
This 'same mould' we can but call the Mystery,
Or rather the 'Darker than any Mystery',
The Doorway whence issued all Secret Essences."
(Chapter I)

Figure 24–2
Barred spiral nebula
NGC 1365.

The first chapter of *Tao Te Ching* has been known for centuries as
a difficult teaching. For that every reason, I will interpret it casually
here, using my *qi* intuition. My restatement of the chapter would go
something like this: Tao is not something that you can always define.
Look, I am able to attain the stage of Nothingness any time I want,
and I am able to become one with everything in the outer world. You
give them names; in doing so, you assume that you know them well.
Can't you see that this is a mistake? All things have existed constantly
from the beginning, long before they had names. By giving things names,
you set them as a general idea in your mind and distinguish yourself
from them.

If you want to see their ultimate truth, stop separating yourself from
them, and become one with them. At the same time, however, you must
know the difference between yourself and other things, keeping the
self separate. These two views can be seen as Yin and Yang. You need
both to comprehend all things. This duality also indicates the function
of Tao. In Tao, you can go further and further for its origin. In Tao,
anyone can realize "who I am," or learn the nature of the self. Therefore, learn the law of nature—that is, Tao!

If you consider the two views, consisting of the inner essence and
outer aspects, as the vibration of all things and the particles of all

things, it will be easier to understand. Or, you can substitute for these two views the concepts of the *qi* of all things and the physical substance of all things. Chapter I of *Tao Te Ching* is full of meaning and only someone who embodied Nothingness, like Lao-Tzu, could ever have described it. There are male and female, day and night, inside and outside, truth and false or hot and cold. The Yin and Yang act on each other, and develop by being opposed to and pulling against each other. The mechanics of this friction is the ultimate principle of creation.

In *qigong*, it is important to look at the inner essence of all beings. If, after mastering the Macrocosmic Orbit method, you are able to do this, you will enter the world of the Transcendental Orbit method.

Nothingness and Physics

Physicist Fritjof Capra became very well known for his work *The Tao of Physics*, in which he argued that "Being itself is the product of Not-being," a concept which is common to the laws of nature as described by by Lao-Tzu and modern quantum theory. At this point I would also like to introduce the views of Japanese physicist Saburo Honma, from his book *Busshitsu no kyukyoku wa nan daro* (What is ultimate matter?), in order to show how much frontier physics has advanced.

"Although no electron exists in Nothingness, an electron can exist if energy is provided. Thus, Nothingness, i.e., Not-being, is potentially able to transform Being. From this view, Nothingness is one manifestation of Being. As the Buddhists say, 'Form is Emptiness and Emptiness, form.' In other words, the phenomenal world, consisting of form, is equivalent to Not-being, and that Not-being is equivalent to the phenomenal world.

"Suppose an atom is as large as a dome the size of an Olympic stadium. There, an atomic nucleus would be the size of an egg, and a few electrons even smaller than a grain of rice. It would look almost 'empty.' However, this 'emptiness' can be considered as a dense space with transient electrons and transient positive electrons (anti-particles), which can give birth to electrons and positive electrons, only if energy is provided from the outside [Figure 24–3].

"At the beginning of the universe and the ultimate of matter, one of the latest theories in physics is that the universe, or matter, was given birth from Nothingness. According to this theory, in the world of Nothingness, where nothing spatiotemporal exists, immeasurably tiny space-time with inexhausible energy keeps appearing and disappearing. Time-space called the 'baby universes' potentially grows into future universes. It can be hypothesized that our universe happened to survive by the tunnel effect, when one of the 'baby universes' was passing through the wall of energy. The surviving "baby universe" developed to this physical world."

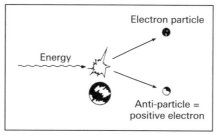

Election generated from vacuum

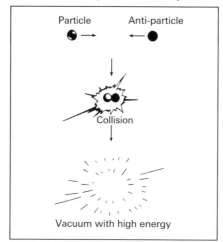

Collision between particles and anti-particles

Figure 24–3
Reaction of particles and anti-particles.

The Ultimate Truth

I mentioned Nothingness in the context of the ninth stage of the Ten Stages of the Development of the Mind (see page 132). In one word, if you want to attain ultimate Nothingness, you must be away from the ordinary consciousness that consists of information from the five senses. Then all waves in the sea of illusion can become tranquil. In this state you can comprehend the true essence of the self.

However, according to Kukai, this stage is not enough! He insists that the ninth stage is still only a beginning level. I wonder what Lao-Tzu and Kukai would say if they discussed this point, but I will wait for another chance to comment on the topic.

It seems that Capra knew of Lao-Tzu but was not familiar with the teachings of Kukai. To Kukai, Nothingness was not what developed from cosmology, but represented the stage before the ultimate enlightenment. If you are familiar with Yoga, you may have noticed that the ninth stage is exactly the same as the definition of Yoga given in *The Upanishads*. As Tsuruji Sahota has noted: "When the five sensory senses stop their function and the judging mind stops its function as well, people call it the ultimate state. To control the organs of the body is regarded as Yoga."

Chuang-Tzu (B.C. 368–290), who ranks with Lao-Tzu, described this as Zuo-wang, or "Transcendental Forgetting": If one drops all the worldly matters, including "forgetting" the body and the body-function, one can unite with the Transcendental Way. Needless to say, Kukai knew of the existence of Lao-Tzu, Chuang-Tzu, and Yoga. Yet he insisted that the ninth stage was far from the tenth stage—that is, from the deepest and most sacred stage. Why? Unfortunately, this question lies beyond the scope of this book. I would like to introduce here one more verse by Kukai, written at the Buddhist ceremony of Ten Thousand Flowers and Lights on Mount Koya in 832.

> Until the universe comes to an end,
> Until all is dead and gone,
> Until the world falls into decay,
> My desire for compassion never fades away.

Figure 24–4

"The mind is an aggregate of photons produced constantly in the left brain tissue with a special emphasis on memory function. Consciousness is the physical movement described by the quantum theory of a field." This is the conclusion drawn from the new theory of the brain and mind known as "quantum brain dynamics" which was pioneered by Japanese physicists Hiromi Umezawa and Yasushi Takahashi and is described in Jibu and Yasue's *No to kokoro no ryoshiron*.

While you practice *qigong*, an unexpected light can sometimes be sensed when you are photographed. No one has ever been able to explain this before. But when I came across this latest theory—that is, that the mind is photons—I thought, why couldn't energy be photosensitive; after all, energy is deeply related to the function of mind known as *qi*. Of course, I don't mean to claim that these photograph serve as proof of the existence of *qi*, but they does mean a great deal to me. I hope that they will also suggest to you how wide and vast are the unexplored spaces of the *qi* world.

I have written about Emptiness, Nothingness, and the essence of our predecessors. These concepts are not difficult to understand. Practice *qigong* persistently and diligently. Someday you will experience a very special state. It might be like being veiled in light, with the self located nowhere in particular. You may be in a state where you become one with your surroundings while also realizing that no such state exists. Then only your mind will exist as mind. You will perceive that your mind exists not only here, but everywhere. This may be a stage that combines local presence and omnipresence. It is not the result of a play of fancy, but is achieved by extending phenomena of the mind as energy.

As long as you keep practicing the Microcosmic and Macrocosmic Orbit methods, the Transcendental Orbit method, and *samadhi*, the gate for the ultimate truth is open to you.

REFERENCES CITED

ENGLISH

Hakeda, Yoshito S., trans. *Kukai: Major Works, Translated with an Account of His Life and a Study of His Thought*. New York: Columbia University Press, 1972.

The Sivananda Yoga Center. *Sivananda Companion to Yoga*. New York: Simon & Schuster, 1983.

Wilber, Ken. *No Boundary: Eastern and Western Approaches to Personal Growth*. Boston and London: Shambhala, 1985.

Whitton, Joel L. , M.D., Ph.D., and Fisher, Joe. *Life Between Life: Scientific Explorations into the Void Separating One Incarnation from the Next*. New York: Doubleday, 1986.

Waley, Arthur, trans. *The Analects of Confucius*. London: George Allen & Unwin, 1938.

—— *The Way and Its Power: A Study of the Tao Te Ching and Its Place in Chinese Thought*. London: George Allen & Unwin, 1934.

JAPANESE

Honma, Saburo. *Busshitsu no kyukyoku wa nan daro* [What is ultimate matter]. Tokyo: Kodansha, 1989.

Jibu, Mari, and Yasue, Kunio. *No to kokoro no ryoshiron* [Quantum theory of the brain and mind]. Tokyo: Kodansha, 1998.

Sahota, Tsuruji. *Yoga sutora* [Yoga sutra]. Tokyo: Hirakawa, 1980.